If My People

by Sun Fannin with Larry Fannin

If My People

by Sun Fannin with Larry Fannin

 Unless otherwise identified, Scripture quotations are from The King James Version of the Bible.

Companion Press
P.O. Box 310
Shippensburg, PA 17257-0310

ISBN 1-56043-500-3

For Worldwide Distribution
Printed in the U.S.A.

Foreword

by Tommy Reid

Ever since I had the privilege of ministry in Korea with Dr. Paul Yonggi Cho in 1961, I have had a great interest in the disciplines of the Korean church, especially as related to fasting and prayer. However, often when a Korean Christian comes to America and attempts to convey the importance of fasting and prayer to our Western culture, we have a tendency to relate these practices primarily to their Eastern culture. We often feel as though our Western schedules and lifestyles are much too busy for these disciplines to really "work" in the American church.

Our friends, Sun Fannin and her husband, Larry, now present to the American Christian the true benefit of fasting and prayer. As you read their story, you will realize that Sun is a Korean by birth, and thus understands the Korean culture and the Korean Christian disciplines. But she is now living in an American culture, married to an American pastor, and is involved in the full pressures of our American society. Understanding our culture fully, she is able to present the message of prayer and fasting out of her own personal experiences in what the Holy Spirit accomplished in her life. She has been healed, released from bitterness, healed of the memory of past sins, and received many other tremendous spiritual victories in this way.

Sun and Larry Fannin's book is one that every Christian should read. I recommend this book and their ministry to you. It will challenge you to a more Biblical form of life as taught to us and practiced by our Lord.

Our lives will be changed, as was the life of Sun Fannin through developing a truly Biblical lifestyle that includes the disciplines of fasting and prayer.

Respectfully submitted,
Rev. Tommy Reid, Pastor
Full Gospel Tabernacle
Orchard Park, NY

Acknowledgments

First of all, much thanks and appreciation to my dear husband Larry who understands, loves and encourages me more than anybody on the earth. Somehow he lets me believe that I can do anything I decide to.

Loving appreciation to my son's Jody and Tejay who sacrificed so much of their time with me to write my book, and my stepson Tony who did the design, typesetting, and production of the book.

Special thanks to my mom, who loves me with her whole heart and patiently prays for me to fulfill what God's call on my life is to do.

Sincere thanks to my good friends: Constance Steindam, Sarah Richardson, Linda Sanders, Pam Steele, Jane Day, Susan Hutson, and many others who gave themselves and their time so freely in their busy schedules to fulfill what was lacking in my ability to finish this book.

Most of all, glory, honor and praise to our Lord Jesus Christ, from whom all healing come.

Sun Fannin

Preface

As I travel around the country speaking in many places, I see many hurt and wounded people. Even among Christians.

I felt the need to write another book with simple, basic guidelines on how we can be healed through prayer and fasting.

God has done so many wonderful things in my life and through them He has taught me how to help others to receive healing for their emotional hurts and wounds.

"If my people" is the condition that God requires from us. If we humble ourselves; if we pray; if we will turn from our own ways; if we will seek His face, then God will hear and God will heal.

This is the first book that my husband Larry and I have written together. We trust that you will learn to know God and learn to walk in His ways, for that is our prayer for everyone who reads this book.

Sun Fannin

CONTENTS

*Chapters written by Larry Fannin
All other chapters written by Sun Fannin

CHAPTER 1

Common misconceptions about fasting

In the Bible we see through fasting and prayer the power of God is released. Yet the majority of Christians today do not fast on a regular basis and even some wonder if it is God's will for them to fast. Fasting is very seldom taught today and some even say fasting is not important. It is not a matter of whether or not we should fast or wait until God lays a burden on our heart to fast. Fasting should be a part of our Christian discipline like prayer and Bible study. The sixth chapter of Matthew teaches us to pray, give alms and to fast, doing it in secret unto God who will give us a reward and blessing. Fear and misconception about fasting are the results of the lack of teaching. The truth about fasting and prayer will set you free and give the reward of the Lord openly for all to see.

Let's look at some misconceptions about fasting.

Misconception 1: "I will die if I don't eat."

Fasting is not starvation and will not hurt the body *if* it is done with common sense and according to the Word of God.

Use wisdom, because your body belongs to the Lord and He does not want us to hurt it.

The body can not live without air more than a few minutes nor without water or sleep but for a few days. But in normal circumstances, the body can live satisfactorily without food for several weeks.

Misconception 2: "How can I know if I am hurting my body?"

Having an understanding of some of the not-so

pleasant symptoms that sometimes occur during the first few days of a "prolonged normal fast" may help reassure you. Often we go through stages during our fast which may overlap and vary in duration with each individual. It is also possible that none of these symptoms are experienced by the person fasting.

Usually we go through four stages of fasting.

First Stage: You will experience a strong craving for food which may last about two or three days. We eat out of habit most of the time; not because we need food or because we are hungry.

Second Stage: You may experience weakness during this stage. This is the most difficult part of the fast and will take faith and determination to go on.

Some of the symptoms commonly experienced are:

- Unpleasant taste in your mouth
- Coated tongue and bad breath
- Headaches
- Dizziness
- Nausea
- Chills
- Sleeplessness
- Pains or cramps in the muscles

These symptoms are partly a result of waste products being cleansed out of the body. Drinking plenty of water will help. After two or three days they should disappear.

One of the major reasons why many do not fast today is because of their lack of knowledge concerning this part of the fast. When they become weak, experience dizziness or have a headache, they are afraid of hurting themselves and break the fast. They allow fear to come in and think if they continue the fast they will become sick and will not be able to function. This is not so. The fast cannot hurt if done with common sense. Fasting is actually healthy for your body.

Third Stage: This is the easiest part of the fast because we will find renewed strength and very little or no desire for food. You will usually experience this after three days. At this time, you feel you can continue without much difficulty. Many people give up before getting to this stage.

Fourth Stage: This is the termination stage. You will experience the return of hunger after a long fast. This is a sign that the body has used up all the fat and waste products. In certain cases, this may begin at the twenty-first day into the fast, but most people can go forty days. Additional signs are fresh breath, clean tongue and clear urine.

It is very important to distinguish between a craving for food and true hunger.
Jesus fasted forty days and afterward the Bible says he was hungry.

I personally experienced a thirty-day fast with normal activity and could easily have continued on if the Lord would have allowed.

Misconception 3: "The fast has to be a long one to please God."
It is up to you. Unless God tells you how long to fast, you do it as a discipline in your life. Fasting should be led by the Lord. He will set the time and kind of fast that He wants for you. This does not relieve us of our responsibility of self-discipline. We must recognize the need for fasting. The willingness to deny

ourselves and seek God out of a pure heart is so important for us to grow spiritually. It is not important how long we fast, but *that* we fast!

Be led by the Lord; do not look at what others are doing. If someone fasted seven days, this does not mean you should do the same to please God. The important thing is we desire God's will in our fast and we do our fast out of a pure motive.

Misconception 4: "If I fast, God will give me the desire of my heart."

Fasting does not obligate God to fulfill all our desires no matter what they are. The account of David in ***II Samuel 12:19-23*** shows us that David could not change God's will concerning the child that God said would die!

The purpose of fasting is to humble ourselves and deny the flesh so that we may seek God. God does not need to fast, but we do! Fasting does not move God. Fasting moves us into agreement with God. It is not trying to manipulate God to agree with us, but to bring our will into harmony with God.

Fasting is a means of humbling ourselves before God in true repentance, not only through our words but through our actions. It is a means of our total surrender to the Lord.

Misconception 5: "Fasting is not truly beneficial; it's not worth the effort to try."

This is not true. Through fasting, we can receive deliverance from demonic oppression, and both physical and emotional healing. Through fasting, we can break the bondage of habits in our lives that have held us captive for so long. Habits like addiction to food, alcohol, smoking, apathy and procrastination.

The Bible says, "My people are destroyed for the lack of knowledge" and "The truth will make you free," so allow the Holy Spirit, the Spirit of Truth, to teach you about the powerful benefits of fasting, and help you overcome your fears and misconceptions about it.

CHAPTER 2

Important guidelines for fasting

I have learned there are principles of fasting and prayer that are very important for the believer to understand. Here are some do's and don'ts for those who sincerely desire to receive an answer from God.

1. You must have a clear goal and a purpose for your fast.

Without a clear goal, you will become distracted, disinterested, and fail to continue. You need to pray and examine your heart. What is the purpose of your fasting? What are you fasting for?

A. Personal sanctification or consecration?

B. Divine intervention, guidance or blessing from God?

C. Intercession for others?

D. To be free from any bondage in your life?

E. To experience the power of God?

F. To draw near to God?

G. To bring revival in your church, city or nation?

•***Luke 4:*** Our Lord Jesus Christ fasted and prayed 40 days in the wilderness to *prepare Himself for public ministry.*

•***Ex. 34:28:*** Moses fasted 40 days before God when he *received the ten commandments.*

•***Esther 4:15-16:*** The people of Israel fasted and prayed three days that *Queen Esther would find favor* when she appeared before the King that their lives would be spared.

•*Jonah 3:* The people of Ninevah fasted and prayed three days with *repentance for the mercy of God,* so their city would be saved from God's judgment.

•*II Chron. 20:* When the Israelites were surrounded by their enemies they humbled themselves, prayed and fasted *for the deliverance of their nation.*

•*Ezra 8:21:* Ezra declared a fast *for protection and for their safe journey.*

•*II Sam. 3:35:* King David fasted and prayed in *sorrow at the death* of Abner.

•*I Sam. 1:7:* Hannah's desire to *bear a son* brought her before the Lord in prayer and fasting.

Many times in the history of Israel the kings and people fasted and prayed to *repent and receive deliverance.* We also need to know the mind of God about the fast we choose.

2. We must fast for the glory of God, not fast for show unto man.

Matt. 6:16-18: Before we begin to fast, we must learn to come to God humbly and with a proper attitude, not just to appear holy unto man. Our fasting and prayer must be done in secret. The devil will tempt us to fast and pray for show unto man. This grieves the Holy Spirit and will hinder His work in our lives and our blessings will be stolen.

3. We must fast for change in ourselves.

James 4:6: (NIV) "God opposes the proud but gives grace to the humble."

The main purpose of a fast is that our nature be changed. Time must be spent before God repenting for sins and humbly examining ourselves openly and honestly. The Holy Spirit will show us the things we had not recognized. The supernatural power of God causes miraculous changes as we submit to the work of the Holy Spirit.

4. We must not use fasting as a substitute for obedience.

I Samuel 15:22 (NIV) "Does the Lord delight in burnt offerings and sacrifices as much as in obeying the voice of the Lord? To obey is better than sacrifice, and to heed is better than the fat of rams."

Without obedience to the revealed will of God, we will not receive anything from Him. Fasting is not a form of religious works that we can earn merits from God. If you know that you are sinning then fasting will not get God to justify your sin. If you know of anything in your life that is displeasing to God, you must repent of it and obey Him. We must not fast with an attitude of trying to manipulate God. He will not honor our fast if we are not willing to obey His will when He reveals it to us.

5. We must discipline ourselves.

Jeremiah 14:12a (NIV) "When they fast, I will not hear their cry..."

Why would God not listen to their cry? The next verse shows us why. This is what the Lord says about His people:

Jeremiah 14:10a (NIV) "Thus they have loved to wander; they have not restrained their feet..."

While we are fasting, we may become touchy, sensitive or grouchy. Some may become nervous and weak physically. Even when we don't feel like using discipline, emotionally or physically, we must discipline ourselves by bringing our emotions and body into submission to the Holy Spirit.

What good is it for us to fast and seek God if we continue to sin? We need to restrain ourselves from anything that would displease the Lord. We should practice the basic Christian disciplines that all Christians have. They should have a regular Bible study and prayer time. They should have clean speech that is without gossip, criticism, and lies. Basically, disipline should be practiced in every area of your life.

All the men and women of the Bible that were used in a mighty way by the Lord were people who practiced seeking God continually. We should also follow their example.

6. **We must have faith in God.**
   Mark 11:24: (NIV) "Therefore I tell you, whatever you ask for in prayer, believe that you have received it, and it will be yours."

   God is all powerful and Almighty! He does not turn His face away when His children come to Him in prayer. If our faith is as big as a mountain but placed in the wrong thing, we will receive nothing. When we realize we're nothing and our faith is placed in Christ (even if it is the size of a mustard seed) He will remove mountains in our lives. The moment we believe God has answered, we invite the power of God into our life.

These six steps are very important guidelines for the one who sincerely wants answers from God through prayer and fasting.

CHAPTER 3

Released from bitterness through fasting

When I first came to the United States, I had a tremendous problem with my in-laws (from my deceased husband's family). They treated me like I was the black sheep of the family. They were prejudiced toward me and would not accept me the way I was; therefore, I was hurt and somewhat bitter toward them. After marriage of seven years, my husband died. I thought since he was gone I could be okay. A year later, I cried out to God and said, "You have blessed me with a new husband who loves me and the Lord with all his heart. You have been so good to me and all I want is to serve You and give it all to You. Lord, I want You to use me for your glory."

Then the Lord spoke to me, "In order for Me to use you, you must get rid of the bitterness in your heart."

I did not understand what God meant. I said "God, I don't have any bitterness in my heart." Then God showed me I did have bitterness toward my ex-in-laws. I was not angry at them, but I thought as long as they didn't bother me and I didn't bother them, we would be fine. However, every time someone mentioned their name, my heart would start pounding. When I thought about them my stomach churned and I knew something was wrong. I could not accept the fact that I had to forgive them and love them the way I should. In the past, I had prayed and asked the Lord to bless them, but deep in my heart I really did not mean it. God dealt with me, asking "How long are you going to keep this bitterness in your heart?" I admitted I had bitterness, but I did not want to forgive them because I had been so deeply hurt. Then the Lord spoke to me to fast three days, eating nothing, drinking only water.

"Lord, I have never fasted three days before." Then He asked, "How *desperate* are you for me to use you? If you are willing, I am able."

I had already learned that obedience to the Lord is the only way to live a fulfilled life in Christ. As the Lord helped me during those three days, I bought a pretty card I wanted to mail to my ex-in-laws. I wrote a beautiful message inside the card. However on the third day, before I could mail it, I got a phone call from them. Now understand, it had been more than a year since any contact had been made with them. I was not at home. My husband took the message and told me that my ex-mother-in-law had called and wanted to talk to me. Quickly, I picked up the phone and called her. During the time I had fasted, God had broken me enough that I was willing to ask, "Mom, will you please forgive me?" I was amazed I could humble myself to ask her that question.

I said "Let me bring the children to see you so that you might enjoy them." Before I could say anymore, I was weeping uncontrollably. God knew the healing that I needed in my heart, and the tears were evidence that all the bad memories of the past were wiped away.

Then my ex-mother-in-law said to me, "Wait a minute, it wasn't you, it was me!" I was so amazed at what God could do when I was obedient to the word of God to fast and pray. He broke me enough that I could humble myself and tell her I was wrong and it wasn't her fault.

After that, we kept visiting each other. She passed away two years later and I thank God that He gave us those two beautiful years together.

Healing from the pain of abortion through fasting

After I finished my book, "***The Bad Luck Baby***", I could not understand why it was taking so long to find someone to publish it for me. I began seeking God's face for the answer to this question as I was very eager for it to be published.

One night, I attended our local women's meeting. The topic was abortion. I was totally unprepared for what happened. I was not conscious of being hurt by my abortion some years ago. I was not aware it was the same as committing murder. In Korean society, abortion is widely accepted as being normal. I just thought the decision I had made was an unfortunate one.

I knew God had forgiven me for all my sins the day I accepted Him as my Lord and Savior; but for some reason, I could not think or talk about my abortion. I always had an uneasy feeling about what I had done to my baby. Whenever these thoughts came to me, I always told Satan, "Back off! It is all under the blood, and God has forgiven me. I will not receive your guilt and condemnation!" I continued suppressing these thoughts and refused to share this part of my life in my ministry with others. A stirring, which I did not understand, began in my heart. At this meeting, I could not bear to look at the pictures of aborted babies. There were pictures of babies torn into many pieces and some of the six-month babies were placed in trash bags. This sight was devastating and heartbreaking. The pictures reminded me of what had happened so many years ago to my baby, who was also six months old at the time of my abortion. As the pictures were handed to me, I quickly hid them in my Bible, out of my sight. I could not understand these feelings for I thought I had already been healed from this past sin in my life.

As these feelings continued throughout the night and into the next day, I realized something was wrong with my life. I asked God, "What is wrong with me? Why couldn't I look at those pictures? Why did they hurt me so badly?"

All at once, I experienced aching and pain over my entire body. My heart ached with so much pain that I could hardly bear what I was feeling. I asked God why I felt so much unbearable pain. He said, "That is the way your baby felt when you induced the poison into your body to destroy him." I finally realized I had to face the reality that I needed a healing in this area of my life. For the first time in seventeen years, I could admit to God that I had murdered my baby and I cried out to God for His mercy and forgiveness. I never acknowledged the fact that he was a part of me, nor considered him as a human being. The moment it hit me, I started sobbing uncontrollably, as when one grieves when a loved one dies.

I realized I needed a supernatural touch from God. I fasted seven days, mourning and grieving for the sin I had committed. During the seven days of fasting, I came to the place where I could release my baby into God's hands. Also during those seven days, the Lord opened my eyes, showing me something else I was not aware of all those years.

Because I ran away from home when I was nineteen years old, my mother and brother disowned me. I thought I was left with no other alternative than to have an abortion. I knew I would not have emotional or financial support from home, so returning was not an option. He showed me I needed to ask my mother for her forgiveness because I was blaming her for my abortion. After sharing this with her for the first time she willingly forgave me and I forgave her. God also told me to share this with my sons, Jody and Tejay, who also willingly forgave me.

After going through this time and receiving my healing for my sin of abortion, I began to wonder what the baby looked like and how he felt about me. God showed me favor by granting the desire of my heart. I had a beautiful dream one night: In the dream, a couple, whom I did not know, came to me and tapped me on the shoulder and said. "Sun, do you remember you gave a son away seventeen years ago to a foster home?" I said, "Yes." They said, "We are the foster parents." They showed me a teenage boy sitting there waiting for me to come and love him. I looked at him and I noticed he could not look at me. He was just sitting there crying. I did not know what to do. His foster parents comforted me by saying, "He will be alright. You need to go and love him. He is crying for joy because after 17 years you have finally accepted him as a part of you and realized that he has existed." Eventually, I opened my arms, grabbed him and cried and cried. I told him how very sorry I was for what happened and asked him to forgive me. He said, "Mommy, I have missed you. I have been waiting to be part of your life." I looked at his face and patted it and said, "Oh, Honey, your complexion is so beautiful and you look like your cousin, Joshua." We just hugged and loved each other for a while. Then I asked him how they had been treating him and he said, "Fine Mom, they are taking care of me and other children that are here with me."

I introduced him to his brothers, Jody and Tejay, my husband, Larry, his grandmother and other relatives. He said "Hi" to everyone. Then the foster parents came back and said it was time to go. I asked, "Why is it time to go? Why can't we stay together?" They said, "It is not time for you to be together forever." Then, I woke up. The Lord showed me the foster parents were angels raising my aborted baby. In a way, I was seeing my unborn son growing up through my nephew, Joshua, who is the same age and lives near me. Someday, I'll see my unborn son face to face and we'll be together forever. I praise God that He is so faithful to answer us when we earnestly seek His face for a desire in our heart. After this dream, which completed my total healing from the pain of abortion, God opened the door for my book to be published.

CHAPTER 5

Additional healing through fasting

In May, 1988, I conducted a three-day prayer and fasting seminar in a church in Ohio. In my heart, I desired so much to minister effectively to the people. God honored this united fast and I sensed a revival in this church. Again, God faithfully proved Himself to me. He was pleased when His people came humbly before Him seeking His face and turning from their wicked ways.

God used this unworthy servant to bless His people. They shared with me how much I had blessed them and they wanted me to return to the area. They were truly overjoyed by what God had done. It was so beautiful and I left with such thankfulness unto God.

On the way back to Indiana, I tearfully told my traveling companion how good God had been to me and that all I wanted was to worship and to thank Him. She agreed and we worshipped and praised Him together. I felt so good on the inside. I said, with excitement, "Oh God, I'm so happy, so blessed!" I felt like I was the most blessed woman in the whole world. During this time of praise God began to flash my past before me and He took me back to my childhood and my life in Korea.

I remembered what hell I experienced on earth without God in my life. I remembered all the verbal abuse I received while growing up. People said to me, "You're no good; you'll never amount to anything; you're a bad luck child. You can't do anything right, you are always causing trouble in people's lives wherever you go." I received beatings until age nineteen from my brother. Sometimes they were so severe I would pass out. I hated my life so much that I thought I would be okay if I could only escape from my brother's abuse. I ran away from home at nineteen. Leaving home at that age without a good reason was not a usual thing for a Korean family. I met a man and started living with him. I thought this was the man of my dreams. Soon my dream fell apart. He started doing things I thought I had escaped from by leaving home. He started beating and verbally abusing me and tried to get me to do things I cannot describe. I wanted to run from the situation but I couldn't because I was pregnant. I knew better than to return home since my family disowned me the day I left. This so-called man of my dreams, the father of my unborn baby, did not claim to be the father. My life went on with such misery. I continued the pregnancy without proper food or clothing. This man used what money we had to get drunk and did not take care of my needs.

I tried to commit suicide because my life was so miserable. I thought I would kill myself so I would not have this baby and would spare it what I had gone through in my life. Two attempts at suicide did not succeed. After six months of pregnancy, I came to a place where I thought there was no other way except to have an abortion. Soon after the abortion the father and I broke up. I went to live with my sister Ann and tried to straighten out my life. I bought new clothes, make-up and fixed my hair. I tried to fix myself so I would look pretty but twenty years of my life had been damaged severely, especially the last year while I lived with this man. No matter how much I fixed up, I could not see myself as pretty or smart enough to do anything. I felt filthy and dirty and believed that I could not live a normal life after what I had done. There was continued nagging in my head, "You're no good. You cause nothing but trouble in people's lives. The man you thought would make your dreams come true told you the same thing. You're no good." That nagging went on day and night and I couldn't control myself.

I started drinking to drown out the nagging. I also started looking for a job. I looked at a private club (like a bar to serve drinking men). Since I felt I was not good enough to find a normal job, I thought this was the only place that would accept me. I got a job the first day I interviewed. I worked there a few days making good tips, so I thought, "no matter what, I'm going to make enough money to live on my own."

After a few days on the job, I went in one afternoon as usual to work. Just as I tried to enter, the owner, who was sitting in the yard, yelled at me, "Stop! Stop! Don't come in." I couldn't understand why she said that! Then I noticed the salt sprinkled on the walkway and right away knew it was used to break curses according to Korean superstition. I was puzzled. The owner came to the door where I was standing. I asked her why I couldn't go in. She informed me that ever since I worked there the business had gone down. She did not want me to work there anymore. Then, she picked up a bowl of salt and sprinkled it on me to break all the curses and bad luck that came out of me to the business. She forced me to leave. The owner spit on me, showing her disgust toward me. She felt I was the cause of all the damage in the business. I did not realize anything was wrong because I did not have any knowledge of how things were before I started working there.

I was humiliated knowing I not only caused trouble in peoples lives but also in a business, I felt there was no hope. I saw only pitch black darkness before me and felt my future was closed. I walked out of the alley to the street. I could hardly see anything or anybody. All I could do was sob and cry for help, wondering if there really was any hope for me. "Is my life over? Can anybody say I want you, I need you, you'll be okay?"

Then I looked around at the people who were passing by me and wondered whether or not these passing people wanted me. "Can anybody tell me that they want me?" It was a horrible experience as I felt I was truly worthless and only caused trouble for everyone that came in contact with me.

Until this moment, almost twenty years later, I had forgotten this episode in my life. Even when I wrote my book, ***The Bad Luck Baby,*** I did not remember this particular part of my life. Now, in amazement I think how God had blessed me with so many people. Wherever I go, people tell me, "We want you, we need you, we love you, please come back." Not only was I blessing individuals but also whole congregations. This was totally opposite of what I had been used to hearing years ago. All of this changed after I committed myself to God. God opened my eyes to show me how He had changed everything for me. This is just the beginning. God will do more as I continue to bless Him with worship and praise and be faithful to Him through obedience.

For the first time in almost twenty years, God took me back to that incident to let me feel the pain of rejection and show me how I needed to forgive these people for what they had done to me. I was driving and at the same time sobbing uncontrollably telling my friend next to me what God had just shown me. I verbally confessed to forgiving these people, asking God to bless them. After all of this, the overwhelming joy of the Lord bubbled through me. I wanted to love Jesus even more and please Him more than anything else. I committed myself to God to do just that. As long as I live, His name will be exalted in my life.

Several months later, in September, 1988, another healing took place in my life. Another one of my sisters and her family moved to the United States from Korea and settled in Indianapolis. We had been separated for many years, and had a lot to share with each other. As I inquired about the rest of the family still in Korea, my sister Punny told me how my oldest sister Cha felt toward me. Punny was telling me about things that had happened fifteen years ago and how Cha was still harboring hurt and anger toward me. At one time I invited Cha and her family to come to the United States and she refused to come. I could not understand why she had resentment toward me. I was not aware of what had been going on in her heart or that she felt this way until now. After our conversation, I was upset in knowing how Cha felt about me after all these years. I wished I could help her but she was in Korea. I did not understand why Cha was not forgiving toward me. At this point, I became angry. I had resentment toward her and I was unable to sleep. The next day, as anger mounted in me, many thoughts started dancing in my head. God then reminded me of an incident in Korea. While in Korea, I was living with an American G.I. (whom I later married). My family heard about it and Cha came to see me one day. She asked me to come outside to talk to her. She would not come in because she considered my house was unclean, at the time, since many Koreans considered that anyone living with an American G.I. was a prostitute. If she came into our house she would be condoning what I was doing. As we stood outside, she started telling me unbearable things. She told me to go away somewhere and never return because I had disgraced the family and placed shame on her life. Because of my living with this American G.I., her husband Kim had been mistreating Cha and accusing her of being like me. Kim would beat her and abuse her verbally when he was drunk. She could no longer continue with this life. She was so angry because I was causing trouble in her life that she pushed my head into a brick wall, hitting me, and told me again, "Get out, go somewhere, so we can never see you or hear about you again."

According to Korean tradition, we were supposed to respect our elders no matter how old we were so I could not fight back. I took it from her. I was crying uncontrollably, not because I was hurt physically, but because I felt so lonely and rejected. I came to the realization that I had nobody. All I could say was that I was sorry. She left. I had to do something about it, so I moved to the country and did not see her until I left to come to the United States.

As God opened my eyes, all at once I felt all the old feelings of hurt and rejection. Anger and resentment rose up in me and I said loudly, "She had no right to be mad at me. I hate her for what she did to me back in Korea." I was so surprised at what I saw in myself because I loved my family and felt that I had forgiven them all. But this caused me to realize I needed more healing in my heart, so I fasted for a week asking God to heal me of the rejection and help me to forgive her.

During this time of fasting, God revealed another incident with my second oldest sister, Ann, who raised me after I returned home from the orphanage. While I was growing up, my mother worked all the time. My family was so poor with seven of us. We hardly had possessions after the Korean War. There was so much hate toward one another; hate toward the world and the life we were living because of the daily hardship we faced. The whole family was having trouble coping. Ann tried to raise me and my other sisters but it was not easy for her. Ann hated it when we would go out and get in trouble with other kids. My sister would paddle us out of her anger and frustration. We never told our mother about these paddlings because it would upset her.

We had no bathroom in the house. Once a month, my sister Punny and I walked five miles to get a bath at the hospital where my mother worked. Mother gave us a bath in the laundry room. Mother could see the bruises on our bodies and she would ask us where they came from. We would not tell her. This happened several times and soon mother figured it out. When she came home, she released her frustration out on Ann. It was so hard on my mother that she passed out from the stress.

Ann was so miserable. She could not take any more pressure so she decided to kill herself by drinking poison. One day when I was six years old she asked me, "What would you do if I died?" I said, "I would die with you." Then she took the lid off the poison saying, "This life is hell to me and I don't want to live anymore. You said if I die you would die with me. We will take this drink and we lay down and sleep, and we will never return to this world." At six years old I did not understand about death, but I felt something was bad and I felt like I had been the cause of all her bad feelings. I begged her that I would be good for I did not want to die. So, she decided not to do it and put the poison away.

About a year later, life had grown worse. Ann still had the poison and she asked me again to die with her. Again, I begged her not to because I was afraid. She never attempted this again. She married a few years later and left home.

During this fast, I received more healings from the past, and God helped me to forgive my sisters. God also helped me to release all the resentment and guilt I had. Unknowingly, deep in my heart, I had felt that I had been the trouble in my sisters life and that I was the reason sister Ann wanted to die, and sister Cha had been mistreated by her husband. After my fast was over, in amazement I asked God, "Am I not totally healed? Are there things in my life that still need to be delivered and healed?" God spoke to me, "I will not allow anything you cannot handle. Whenever I see you're ready for more, then in My time it will be done."

ICorinthians 10:13 (NIV) "No temptation has seized you except what is common to man. And God is faithful; he will not let you be tempted beyond what you can bear. But when you are tempted, he will also provide a way so that you can stand up under it."

There are things in the past some people are not ready to face. I praise God for His unfailing faithfulness and mercy to finish the work He started in my life.

Philippians 1:6 (NIV) "Being confident of this, that he who began a good work in you will carry it on to completion until the day of Christ Jesus."

I know if there are more healings to come from my past, I will not be afraid to face them because I know God is with me all the way! After these seven days of fasting and healing, God allowed me to talk to Ann, who now lives in Indianapolis. I made things right with her. He also allowed me to return to Korea in February, 1989, at which time Cha and I were healed through God's grace.

CHAPTER 6

Set free from unforgiveness

In counseling and praying with people we have found that many emotional problems people are facing today are the result of bitterness and unforgiveness.

Many have been hurt deeply and treated so unfairly that it is extremely difficult to forgive. God says that we must forgive.

Matthew 6:14-15 (NIV) "For if you forgive men when they sin against you, your heavenly Father will also forgive. But if you do not forgive men their sins, your Father will not forgive your sins."

Our freedom and peace depends on the forgiveness that we have received from God by grace. Since we have been forgiven by God, then we are required to forgive all others who have hurt us.

Hebrews 12:15 (NIV) "See to it that no one misses the grace of God and that no bitter root grows up to cause trouble and defile many.".

If we refuse to forgive others, then we can miss the grace of God. Whatever God asks us to do, He also gives us the grace to do it.

Unforgiveness is like acid; it will eat and destroy the peace and joy in our soul. Unforgiveness causes us to live under the heaviness of guilt and condemnation. Unforgiveness may cause many physical problems: headaches, ulcers, indigestion, nervousness and sleeplessness. These symptoms are not worth the toil they take on your body.

When we hold on to the hurts, we can hinder God from healing us. We lose our sweet communion with the Lord Jesus because our thoughts are occupied with the offender and the offenses inflicted on us.

We can be free from all this torment, but there is a price to pay.

Luke 9:23 (NIV) "Then He said to them all: "If anyone would come after me, he must deny himself and take up his cross daily and follow me."

First: We have to die to self and to all of our rights. Accept God's will, which is to forgive as we have been forgiven. It is not a matter of who is right or who is wrong. What matters is the will of God. We must choose to forgive, and be willing to obey God. If we are willing, God is able to give us the grace to do it.

Through prayer and fasting we can accomplish the yielding of our will to the will of God. The purpose of fasting is to humble ourselves, deny the flesh, and invite the power of the Holy Spirit into our hearts. When we fast and pray humbly before God, our old carnal nature is crucified, and the power of the Holy Spirit is free to be manifested in our lives. We are responsible for our actions. Fasting is a means of true repentance, not only through our words, but through our actions. It is a means of total dependence and faith to let the Lord do the work in our lives, whatever that would be.

The main purpose of fasting is that our nature be changed. We must clean out every type of sin in our lives that has been hindering our relationship with the Lord Jesus Christ. The sins of unforgiveness, bitterness, hate, resentment, anger, revenge, retaliation and disobedience.

Joel 2:12-13 (NIV) "Even now, declares the Lord, return to me with all your heart, with fasting and weeping and mourning. Rend your heart and not your garments. Return to the Lord your God, for He is gracious and compassionate, slow to anger and abounding in love, and he relents from sending calamity."

The supernatural power of God will miraculously change and heal us as we humble ourselves and honestly seek Him with fasting and prayer. Our responsibility is to forgive those who have hurt or abused us, and allow God to do His work in our hearts and theirs.

When we forgive, we must forgive unconditionally! So often we say "Well, I will forgive, but I won't forget." Or we say "I will forgive if she/he apoligizes first." This is conditional forgiveness and only partial. Other times we are silent toward a person, but we are really punishing them with our silence. This again, is far from forgiveness. We are shouting inwardly, "This is the price you must pay for my forgiveness." Just as God's love is freely given (without price-tags) so is forgiveness. Jesus' forgiveness is without any strings, without any condition. Jesus is no respecter of persons. He loves and forgives anyone who asks and receives Him. If we are to follow His example, our love and forgiveness must also be given freely.

1 John 3:16 (NIV) "This is how we know what love is: Jesus Christ laid down his life for us. And we ought to lay down our lives for our brothers."

Ephesians 4:32 (NIV) "Be kind and compassionate to one another, forgiving each other, just as in Christ God forgave you."

Please, don't waste your life worrying about what has happened in the past, or trying to get even.

Romans 12:19 (NIV) "Do not take revenge, my friends, but leave room for God's wrath, for it is written: "It is mine to avenge; I will repay," says the Lord."

I know by my personal experience that God is always faithful to perform beyond our own human limitations. It does not matter how impossible it looks or how deeply you are hurt, I know that God is able. God has proven Himslef faithful in my own life time and time again.

How *desperate* are you to become free and stay free? Do you really want God's peace and joy? Are you tired of living in your bondage? Then I ask you choose NOW God's will for you, which is to forgive.

Second: We must change our focus from the hurt (and the one who hurt us), and put our thoughts toward God and his grace.

Bitterness consumes our thoughts and our energy. We will end up physically sick and mentally depressed.

One way of telling if a person is bitter is by what they talk about. If they keep bringing up the hurt and going over it with anyone who will listen, they are not yet healed.

Luke 6:45 (KJV) "A good man out of the good treasure of his heart bringeth forth that which is good; and an evil man out of the evil treasure of his heart bringeth forth that which is evil: for of the abundance of the heart the mouth speaketh."

If we have forgiven, then we need not talk about it anymore. Unforgiveness will cause us to become critical towards the person and see them only in a negative way. The bitterness will affect our whole life. We will be insecure and overly sensitive. Worst of all, we lose our sense of peace with God. It affects our judgment so that we may make poor decisions.

As a friend of mine once said "Pain is inevitable but misery is an option." We personally know people who are bitter; they are miserable to be around and they have aged beyond their years. They are in poor health, and are bound by depression. The bitterness comes out of their mouth everytime we see them. But they will not change; they have chosen to keep their unforgiveness. We also know many who were deeply hurt and yet by the grace of God they forgave. Now, they are prosperous and happy people in the Lord.

Third: We need to see the spiritual forces that are involved.

Ephesians 6:12 (NIV) "For our struggle is not against flesh and blood, but against the rulers, against the authorities, against the powers of this dark world and against the spiritual forces of evil in the heavenly realms."

Not only are people involved in our bitterness and unforgiveness but the devil takes advantage of the situation as an opportunity to cause more suffering.

God loves the sinner but hates the sin. We also need to love the person even though we do not like what they have done.

Once we have forgiven, then we have the power and authority released in us by the Lord Jesus Christ to use His name against all demonic force.

Luke 10:17 (NIV) "The seventy-two returned with joy and said, "Lord, even the demons submit to us in your name."

We must use the authority that has been given to us to put our enemies under our feet. The devil motivates people against us through persecution and prejudice. If we live a godly life, we will at times suffer persecution from others.

II Timothy 3:12 (NIV) "In fact, everyone who wants to live a godly life in Christ Jesus will be persecuted."

Sad to say, but sometimes even our own Christian brothers and sisters allow the devil to use them. They may not realize it at the time, but it does happen.

When we pray, we should bind and rebuke the evil spirits and do spiritual battle like Daniel did (read Daniel Chapter 9-10). More is accomplished through fasting and prayer than we can see with our eyes.

Once the bondage of unforgiveness is broken in us, we will experience God's peace and joy in our hearts.

Our confidence in who we are, and who our God is will increase because of what He has done in us as we have been obedient to Him.

Fourth: Jesus gave us the formula for freedom.

Matthew 5:43-44 (NKJV) "You have heard it was said, 'you shall love your neighbor and hate your enemy.' But I say to you, *love* your enemies, *bless* those who curse you, *do good* to those who hate you, and *pray* for those who spitefully use you and persecute you."

Jesus said that we are to:

1. Love them.
2. Bless them.
3. Do good to them.
4. Pray for them.

Without God's grace it would be impossible for us to do this. We are human. Our natural desire is to strike back and get revenge. If you think about it, our feelings of hate do not hurt them; it hurts us. We are the ones who suffer the most. For our own good we need to forgive. Unforgiveness is like having a dead weight chained and dragging behind us.

How can we do this? Where do we start?

First, begin by praying for them. It may be hard at first but keep at it.

Second, when you pray, ask God's forgiveness for the evil thoughts and words that you have towards them.

Third, name him/her and forgive them. Say each name out loud.

Forth, ask God to take out the hurts. Replace it with love for them.

Fifth, ask God to bless them. Everytime the hurtful thoughts try to come back, say this out loud *"I bless them and I will not curse them."* Then pray *"God bless them and curse them not."*

If we will stay with it, God's grace and power will work in us and gradually our hearts will heal. The time will come when you don't have to work at it anymore because it comes naturally, from your heart.

I knew when I had truly forgiven those who had hurt me, as God put love in my heart for them. I stopped wishing evil on them, and actually prayed for them, asking God to bless them. ***What a freedom!*** What a great feeling to be right with God! It is worth paying the price!

CHAPTER 7

Healing of the soul through fasting

by Larry Fannin

Isaiah 58:6 (NKJV) "Is this not the fast that I have chosen: To loose the bonds of wickedness, to undo the heavy burdens, to let the oppressed go free, and that you break every yoke?"

Some of the blessings of fasting and prayer are; the healing of the soul, deliverance from demonic oppression and release from the effects of past hurts that have wounded our emotions.

Fasting brings us into a position with God so the Holy Spirit can remove the bondage in us that is the result of the bruises of Satan.

The bruises of Satan are the wounds in our emotions as a result of hurts inflicted upon us through circumstances and people.

Ephesians 4:27 (NKJV) "Nor give place to the devil." The word "place" also means opportunity, occasion, opening, or foothold. The wounds to our emotions are like a wound to our body that causes a cut. The wound can become infected (demonic oppression), and sore (sensitive, hurts each time it's bumped), and may cause us a lifetime of reoccuring pain. Through fasting and prayer, the Holy Spirit will cleanse and heal the wound. Time is not a healer as some say. If emotional wounds are not healed, they don't get better; they grow deeper and cause other forms of emotional problems.

Emotional wounds don't *work out* in time; they *work in* us producing all kinds of roots that produce the fruits of mental torment and open us up for demonic oppression.

Hebrews 12:15 (NKJV) "looking diligently lest anyone fall short of the grace of God; lest any root of bitterness springing up cause trouble, and by this many may become defiled."

Satan's goal is to *bruise* our emotions so that he may *blind* our minds, that he may *bind* our will, in order to gain a measure of control over us and eventually destroy our lives. The soul of man, which is his mind, will and emotions, were designed by God to be the servant of the Spirit when it is healed and under control of the Holy Spirit. If our mind, will or emotions are wounded or bound, then our ability to hear and serve God is dramatically affected. God's will is that we come to a wholeness that produces holiness, which is the image and character of Christ.

I Thess. 5:23-24 (NKJV) "Now may the God of peace Himself sanctify you completely; and may your whole spirit, soul, and body be preserved blameless at the coming of our Lord Jesus Christ. He who calls you is faithful, who also will do it."

Satan can only take advantage of our negative reactions to the pain inflicted upon us through people or circumstances. It's not people or circumstances that cause the root problems in us, it is how we react to them.

Rejection is the root of almost all emotional problems and produces the fruit of stunted spiritual growth, emotional instability and demonic oppression. Two other problems result from rejecton: 1. self-rejection, an inner wound (what happens in us), and 2. fear of rejection an outward reaction (how we relate to others).

Three Aspects of Rejection:

1. Symptoms:

a. Easily hurt; over sensitive; touchy.

b. Resentment; bitterness; a critical, judgmental attitude.

c. Distrust of others; withdrawal from relationships; feeling like the whole world is out to hurt them.

d. Isolation; selfishness; self-centered; discrediting others to make themselves look better.

e. Fear of what people will think, so approval is sought through:

1. Dress.
2. Position.
3. Forced religious performance (to appear spiritual).
4. Extremes in doctrine and practices, may be open for occult or cultic teachings; mystical and unrealistic or unpractical behavior.

f. Will do anything good or bad to gain approval of man.

g. Chronic lying; doubtful; skeptical; deep feelings of unworthiness and insecurity.

h. Very low self-esteem; low self-image.

i. Addictions to drugs, alcohol, tobacco, rock music, movies, working long hours as a means to escape reality.

j. Living under the bondage of Murphy's Law; "If anything can go wrong, it will."

2. Source:

The source of rejection usually comes during our childhood. The family is the number one cause of rejection. God's will is for the family to be where we receive love, acceptance, approval and emotional maturity. Children do not just grow up alone like a weed. Children must receive nurturing and proper parental guidance. As children grow up they develop their self-image, moral values and emotional stability through their relationship with their parents. A child will believe everything that a parent says about them. The parent's words and actions, positive or negative, help the child form their self-image.

Proverbs 18:21 (NKJV) "Death and life are in the power of the tongue."

Parents sin against their children, wounding their emotions by the words they *speak*..i.e. "You're no good, Can't you do anything right? Why can't you be like other children, or like your brother, sister, etc? You dummy, what will people think? You're fat, short, tall, different." Children hear their parents conversation with others, like: "He (she) was a mistake. We weren't planning to have a baby. I wanted a boy (or girl). He (she) is a little slow. I don't think they will ever be a success."

Words like these are death to a child. They give the child the information that they use to paint upon the canvas of their soul the picture of themselves.

Parents sin against the child by their *actions*: Divorce and physical or sexual abuse are tragic to the child and the child will blame themselves, not the parents. It is tragic that parents can be so preoccupied with themselves and sin against their children through *neglect*. The child does not understand why the parents do not have time for them. The parents pass on to the child their own emotional problems and produce copies of themselves in their child. Their inability or refusal to give or show love, results in emotional starvation in the child. Later in life, parents are shocked when their children become rebellious and wild. *Things* are no substitute for proper parental love and care.

Some children are blessed with a good home and good parents who give good training, but later in life they may suffer severe rejection through divorce, deep hurt, or broken relationships with people. We *can not* control what happens to us *but we can* control, with God's grace, our reactions to the things that happen to us.

3. Seven steps to freedom:

Each step begins with the letter"**R**" to help you remember.

Step One: Recognize the source.

Whether intentional or not, the source of your hurt is not God, your parents, other people or your circumstance. The source is Satan's bruises and your reactions to the hurt.

James 1:17 (NKJV) "Every good gift and every perfect gift is from above..."

Step Two: Realize what has been wounded.

Your self-image and your feelings of self-worth have been wounded. The lies of Satan have caused you to paint a false self-image. Through fasting and prayer allow the Holy Spirit to reveal those hurts to you. The truth of what the Word of God says will set you free from the lies of Satan that have kept you bound. The renewing of your mind by the Word of God and the Holy Spirit will bring life changing results in your soul.

John 8:32 (NKJV) "And you shall know the truth, and the truth shall make you free."

Step Three: Repent of your sinful responses and take full responsibility for your actions to them. We can not control what other people have done, but we can take responsibility for our actions. Repentance takes away all legal ground for satan's oppression and opens us to Receive God's grace to be healed.

Acts 17:30 (NKJV) "Truly, these times of ignorance God overlooked, but now commands all men everywhere to repent."

Step Four: Release all others from your judgment through forgiveness. Release your resentment and bitterness by choosing to forgive everyone who has ever hurt you. If you are willing to forgive, then God is able to work in you the ability to forgive by His grace.

Ephesians 4:32 (NKJV) "And be kind to one another, tenderhearted, forgiving one another, just as God in Christ also forgave you."

Step Five: Renounce all of Satan's lies in you and break every curse that he has put upon you, through the power and authority of the name of the Lord Jesus Christ. By your mouth close every door to Satan and bind it shut by the blood of Jesus. You have taken away Satan's legal ground to oppress you through repentance and forgiveness and now you must stand upon the truth of God's word.

James 4:7 (NKJV) "Therefore submit to God, resist the devil and he will flee from you."

Step Six: Receive your healing, forgive yourself, and turn from the past. Dare not live in the past but press on towards the fullness of the Lord Jesus Christ and His will for you. Deliverance is a walk. You must realize you will be tested and tempted to return to your old ways. Praise Him daily and confess with your mouth God's healing and victory. Guard your thoughts. You can not afford the luxury of self-pity. You must see yourself in Christ. He is your security and His grace is your ability to continue until you are perfectly whole.

Philippians 4:6 (NKJV) "Be anxious for nothing, but in everything by prayer and supplication, with thanksgiving, let your requests be made known to God."

Step Seven: Reconciliation. Seek to reconcile broken relationships where it is possible. Watch for Satan's deception here. Don't go to anyone until *after* you *know* that God wills it and you are *prepared* through the Holy Spirit to go. *Wait* for God's timing. Not everyone will receive you and not all relationships can be reconciled. Do your part and God will do His. Seek Godly counsel and go slowly. Others can help you see the things you can not see.

IICorinthians 5:18-19 (NKJV) "Now all things are of God, who has reconciled us to Himself through Jesus Christ, and has given us the ministry of reconciliation, that is, that God was in Christ reconciling the world to Himself, not imputing their trespasses to them, and has committed to us the word of reconciliation.

Each person is different and each one must be dealt with individually. This is intended as a guideline. There is so much more to be said that volumes of books could be written on each step.

Godly counsel is encouraged. Sometimes, healing comes slower with some wounds and easier and faster with others. Through fasting and prayer, you will grow in your personal relationship with the Lord Jesus and be changed more and more into His image from Glory to Glory by the Spirit of the Lord.

II Corinthians 3:18 (NKJV) "But we all, with unveiled face, beholding as in a mirror the glory of the Lord, are being transformed into the same image from glory to glory, just as by the Spirit of the Lord."

CHAPTER 8

Deliverance from self-pity through fasting

Once God called me to fast because, for a period of time, I hadn't felt joy or freedom. Many nights I went to bed but couldn't sleep. I was suffering with the feelings of self-pity and hopelessness.

One morning, as I was getting ready for work, I felt very heavy and depressed. I asked God, "Why am I feeling this way?" I thought I had received freedom in my life, but I had no joy. What had I done to lose the joy and the freedom? After arriving at work, I continued to pray. I couldn't concentrate on my work, so I went to the restroom. Since my sister and I were the only women working in the factory, I was not afraid of interuption. I knelt down on the floor and called on God to show me what was wrong. I was so tired of feeling this way; I wanted to be free. As I desperately cried out to God, He gave me these Scriptures: ***Revelation 3:15-16 (NIV)*** "I know your deeds, that you are neither hot nor cold. I wish you were either one or the other! So, because you are lukewarm, neither cold or hot, I am about to spit you out of my mouth." ***Luke 9:23 (NIV)*** "Then He said to them all: "If anyone would come after me, he must deny himself and take up his cross daily and follow me." He revealed to me that I was lukewarm and I needed to put my flesh on the cross. I thought I was fully committed to the Lord, but God showed me that once again I had let flesh come before Him.

This type of sin can creep up on us so easily. At first, we don't notice it. Then, we become miserable because of the consequences of our sins. I didn't want sin in my life and my desire was to please the Lord at all times, in every way. However, I began to notice it was harder for me to praise God, and I didn't seem to care about witnessing to people anymore. I had become spiritually lazy and had not done anything about it. I thought all these emotional feelings were because I was working so hard, and just physically tired.

I asked the Lord what He wanted me to do. He laid on my heart to fast seven days. At first, I thought I could not fast for that long. My job was strenuous. I was working at the factory six days a week, ten hours a day. I needed my strength. But deep inside the truth was I really enjoyed food. Everything tasted good to me, and I didn't want to give up my fleshly desire for food. Then the Lord asked me, "How *desperate* are you to be free, and how much do you want to please me?" I could no longer argue about fasting.

This was the first time I had fasted for seven days drinking only water. As I committed totally to the fast, God took my desire for food away. I was surprised that I could work so hard and keep going all week. When I began feeling weak, I asked the Lord for His strength and He always gave it to me. But, strength is not all the Lord gave me.

The first day, God revealed that the root of my problems were feelings of rejection, and I was suffering from self-pity.

Rejection came into my life as a baby in my mother's womb. My father died during the Korean War, before I was born. My mother was eight months pregnant with me at the time. She already had five children to take care of and she was totally dependent on my father. His death was too great of a shock for my mother. She felt she couldn't handle it. So when I was born, no one in the family welcomed me. Instead of rejoicing, they rejected me. All my family and relatives called me a "bad luck baby." I was blamed for all the bad things that had happened in my family. Because of the hardship of the Korean War and of having six children and no husband, things were so difficult my mother couldn't take care of me anymore. As a result, when I was two years old, my mother gave me to a family for adoption. However, through a miracle of God, I was restored to my mother after three years. Miraculously, as I cried out to God for healing in my heart, God healed and delivered me. Because of being lukewarm, I had to battle with it again. I turned to the Lord in repentance because I had opened the door to feelings of rejection.

On the second day, God showed me that my lack of confidence and my feeling of unworthiness were also a result of rejection. As the Lord caused me to see my true self, I cried out to Him in repentance for this too.

On the third day, **It was victory day!** God healed me and restored His joy in me. I regained my first love. The joy of the Lord strengthened me. It was the third day when I felt the weakest physically, but knowing that I was in His will and obeying Him gave me the strength to carry through.

On the fourth day, the Lord said I would be used to help minister to others with the same problems of rejection and self-pity.

On the fifth day, the Lord gave me the desire to share this testimony in our church newsletter. Usually, I have to write in Korean first, and then translate it into English. This time, the Lord helped me write completely in English. That was truly a new experience for me.

On the sixth day, I felt much closer to God than ever before. He had truly restored me. I realized that I needed to discipline my life and not go according to my feelings. Deliverance is a walk, we must never think Satan has forgotten. We can never take these Scriptures lightly. ***Ephesians 6:10-12; James 4:7-8; I Peter 5:7-8; John 10:10;*** and ***II Corinthians 10:4-5.*** We need to guard our mind, and keep our relationship strong in the Lord. Self-pity is a door opener to all kinds of things with which the devil can deceive us.

On the seventh day, we had a beautiful service at church and I felt everything was wonderful and everyone was beautiful. That was only because *I felt Jesus in full control of my life again.* He is so beautiful and so good! Praise the name of the Lord forever and ever!

CHAPTER 9

Deliverance from fear of man through fasting

In October, 1984, God gave me a dream: In the dream, I saw myself standing in front of a multitude of people, giving my testimony and preaching. When I woke up, I felt good because of what I had seen in the dream. That had always been my desire, to give my testimony and preach about what God had done in my life. However, I did not know how this could be possible.

Being Korean, I lacked self-confidence. While I was growing up, I was always told I was not good enough and I could do nothing right. However, more than anything, I felt I could not speak English well enough to get up in front of people to give my testimony and preach. I feared what people would think when I stood up to say something; that might not make any sense to them.

The dream really stirred and provoked me to cry out to God, "Lord I know you gave me this dream to show me I would someday stand in front of a multitude, give my testimony and preach. But, through my eyes, it seems impossible to fulfill what You have called me to do Lord. I need Your help so I can have the boldness to speak to the multitudes without fear of what they might think of me." A couple of months later, in December, I received my first invitation to speak. I was asked to give my testimony at a local women's meeting to be held in February of 1985. In January of 1985, in our home, we had an intercessory prayer meeting from our local women's meeting. All evening, I felt very impressed to share with these ladies what God had shown me in my dream. At first, I felt like a fool to share something that had not yet happened. However, since I could not shake it off, I opened my mouth and confessed to them. I shared that someday I would get up in front of the multitudes and give my testimony and preach. Everybody rejoiced with me and said, "We are not surprised at all at what God can do through you."

When February finally arrived, I was very anxious for my first speaking engagement. I at last had the confidence to do what I had been called to do. As I stood before the women, my desire to help and serve them replaced any fear and doubt. I became a yielded vessel and God did all the work. I was truly amazed how God had used me to bless the many women that were in the meeting.

In March, I attended another local women's meeting and the speaker ministered to the women who attended. I was amazed to see how this woman could see things in people's lives as she prophesied and ministered. I sat in a corner interceding that all of the people there would receive ministry. Then she called me out and said she saw me standing up in front of the multitudes. She didn't know I was preaching or giving my testimony, but she knew I would be speaking to the multitudes. She said she saw God opening many doors for me beginning in 1985 and continuing until 1988, then she stopped. She spoke with great excitement in her voice. The Lord showed her that in 1988 my name would be spread throughout the nation. It was so amazing to me that God used her to confirm the dream He had given me in the fall of 1984. He assured me without any doubt this would indeed happen. I received the word with great joy in my heart as did my friends, who were in the intercessory prayer meeting, upon hearing of this confirmation. After I fully realized my dream was manifesting itself, an overwhelming fear came over me.

Again, being Korean, I wondered how this could happen. Deep inside, I knew God would use me mightily; however, I could only see myself as a little Korean girl living in a little town, helping my husband pastor a small church. I could not see anything positive about myself, only what I could not do. I was desperately crying out to God to help me overcome my fear of man.

In the summer of 1985, I decided to fast seven days to break from this bondage. During this time of fasting, I heard that the woman (who had prophesied to me in March, 1985) was having a meeting in her home in Indianapolis. I felt led by the Spirit to go to this meeting. I went with several other ladies from our local church. God moved mightily as He had done before and she called me up to pray and prophesy over me.

"You are going through a real battle in your spirit and you've been waiting for the deliverance to come in your life and this night, as you believe with all your heart, God will set you free. You will receive deliverance."

This woman preacher did not even touch me, but I stood with my arms raised swaying back and forth, crying desperately for God to deliver me from this bondage. She asked a couple of the ladies to anoint my feet. As they anointed my feet, I fell under the power of the Holy Spirit. At that moment, there was nothing behind me but a sofa and that is where I fell. After falling on the sofa, still having my hands raised, I started praying in tongues. I realized the awkward position that I was in and I noticed that I was speaking only one word. Normally, I could speak my prayer language fluently, so I tried to change my position and tongues;

however, I could not change or move. I became afraid, thinking I must look foolish and wondering what my local church women were thinking. I continued this way for at least twenty minutes. I asked God,"What is going on?" I could do nothing and I felt so helpless. Then He asked me,"You had tried to move your hands and speak fluently and could not. Who has control over your life to move your hands, to change your position or change your speech?" I answered to Him that He had the power to do it. Then He asked again, "When I let you get up in front of multitudes, is it going to be you or Me working through you?" I said, "It's You." Then the scripture came to me. ***Philippians 4:13 (NKJV)*** "I can do all things *through* Christ who strengthens me." Finally, the truth hit me that I had been full of doubt and unbelief to trust the Lord. If I yield myself to the Holy Spirit, He will be in control and give me the power to do what God has called me to do. That moment I realized I could do nothing, but only by God's power working through me, I was released from my awkward position and could speak normally again. I fell on my face and I repented with true brokenness of being self-centered instead of Christ-centered. I was only thinking of what I could do myself, not what God could do through me. After this true repentance, God healed me from the fear of man.

After this healing, God opened doors for me to speak at many other women's meetings and churches. Then in 1986, God laid on my heart to write a book, ***"The Bad Luck Baby"***, which was published in 1987. In 1988, my name was spread over the nation as prophesy had said, and I stood in front of the multitudes giving my testimony, preaching and teaching about prayer and fasting, as I had dreamed.

In conclusion, I want to say that fasting helped put away the flesh, including my fear of man, allowing the Spirit to rise and take control, and for healing to take place in my life. Obviously, boldness and confidence in the Lord resulted from this particular fast; an experience I will never forget! Glory to God!

CHAPTER 10

Healing of my body through fasting

In December, 1987, I accidentally fell down the stairs and injured my back. I was taken to the hospital where it was confirmed that I had compressed two vertebra. The pain was so intense that I could barely move. I was hospitalized for five days. During that time, the doctor told me the damage was so severe I would be in a body brace for three months. Even after three months, there would be no guarantee I would ever be free of pain, because 90% of these cases can result in arthritis. During that time, I was taking as many pain shots as they would allow me to take, along with pills to calm my nerves.

Being an active person, it was hard for me to accept that I would be immobile for so long and face many physical limitations. At the time, I had been traveling for two years, teaching and giving my testimony at different women's meetings and churches all over the country. I was enjoying what the Lord had me doing. What had happened to my body was a total nightmare! I had such resentment and hatred toward the person who had been very close to me at the time of my fall. I felt it was the person's fault that caused my hurt.

After coming home from the hospital, I asked God to heal me. However, He showed me that I must first forgive this person whom I had the resentment toward. I needed to have mercy on the person as I needed mercy from God for myself. Every time I felt the pain in my body, the more I felt the hatred toward the person. It was so hard for me to forgive. The Lord dealt with me that, to receive total healing for my back, I must first receive healing in my heart. I knew I could not argue anymore with God, so I fasted for seven days. During this time, I stopped taking my medicine and had very little trouble with pain. I asked God to help me forgive the person and heal me of my inward hurts. God gave me His grace abundantly. I no longer thought about my pain, but had mercy on the other person's behalf. I knew God had touched me in a very special way because I could not hate any longer, but found love. The peace and joy of the Lord overwhelmed me as I realized what God had done for me. I knew without doubt I would receive healing for my back. I would be back to normal, as active as ever and even stronger than before.

On the thirteeth day after the accident, I attended a church where they were having a miracle healing service. That night the Evangelist prayed for me and I fell under the power of God. I still had the body brace on, but as I lay on the floor, I felt heat vibrating through my back. I knew that was the healing virtue being released. As I continued to lie there, I knew beyond any doubt in my heart I was truly healed. After I got up, I slowly started to test my back by bending my body and raising my arms, something I could not do before, and I felt absolutely no pain! I tried again, faster and faster. It did not hurt! I started praising God loudly, as I ran back and forth in front of the church, thanking Him for the miracle I had received that night. Full of gratitude, I glorified His Name. On arriving home, I removed the brace.

Two weeks later, I went to the doctor for a check-up. The x-rays showed much improvement, but the doctor did not know I was not wearing the brace, so I told him what had happened. He did not believe me. He could not release me from wearing the back brace, but I knew in my heart that I was totally healed.

The next visit the doctor released me because he saw how beautifully my back was healing. Again, he reminded me not to be surprised if I suffer from arthritis the rest of my life. I praise my God as I was obedient to forgive, and this allowed God to heal my heart. He also healed my back completely as He had promised.

A year after the accident, I had a problem with my knees. Thinking maybe this could be caused from my back injury, someone suggested that I go see a Chiropractor. I went because the pain was great and I did not know for sure the origin of the pain, even though in my heart I knew my back was healed. As I went to the Chiropractor, he took x-rays of my back and he asked me if I had any pain from arthritis. I answered to him that I did not notice any, then I told him about the healing I had received from God. This doctor was a Believer and he had tears in his eyes. He pointed out that the x-ray showed a problem and that I should be in much pain. It was hard for him to understand why I had none. He praised God saying, "God is real and He has given you a miracle." He found no problem coming from my back, but just a twist in my knee from an unknown fall. He treated me for that.

When I visited my family doctor, he continued to ask me if I had a problem with my back. I was always able to tell him"No!" I let him know God had touched me and healed me forever. He said with a smile on his face, "Whoever has healed you, I'm so glad, because you don't have a problem with your back now!"

CHAPTER 11

Disciplining the flesh through fasting

There was a time when God dealt with me to get up early in the morning to spend time with Him. As I am the type of person to stay up all night and sleep all day, I kept putting it off because I thought it would be hard. God kept dealing with me until I became so miserable I told Him I would obey. I realized I had been lazy and this was not pleasing to God. The desire burned deep in my heart to reach my full potential in Christ, so I knew I had to do something about it. I asked God to help me get up early in the morning to spend time with Him. During this time, He put on my heart to fast. I asked Him how many days, but He did not tell me. I started out of obedience not knowing how long to continue. Deep inside, I was disturbed that He had not shown me how long to fast as He had in the past.

This time was different and I did not know what to expect. I started the first day by getting up at six o' clock in the morning and going to my special place to pray. I enjoyed the time with the Lord, praise God!

I got up the second day feeling very sleepy. The first thing I did was to take a shower in order to stay awake. Then, I went to my special place to meet God. I said, "God I'm here to serve, worship and praise You." I prayed on for awhile.

On the third morning, I knew it was six o' clock but I was very tired and sleepy. I asked God to give me five more minutes. He told me to get up, but I couldn't. I was pleading with Him the whole time saying "Just one more minute." This continued for a total of five times before I got up.

It took me fifteen minutes to get up on the fourth morning! And though it took me thirty minutes to get up on the fifth morning, the Lord kept urging me each morning to get up. After putting it off several times, I finally got up and, because I was so tired, I was grumbling, "God, you know I've been fasting and I'm hungry, weak, and sleepy." All kinds of excuses were made. Determinedly, I said, "I'm going to pray, God, *I'm going to pray.*" As I tried to spend time with the Lord, I was not enjoying it.

The sixth morning I fought forty-five minutes with the Lord before I finally got out of bed. Again, as I was walking toward my special place, I was grumbling, "God, I'm tired. This is the sixth day and I'm starving. When will I be released from this fast?" I sat down having a nonchalant attitude while praying in the Spirit, in English and in Korean. I prayed and prayed but it seemed like it was not going anywhere. I asked, "God, where are you?" It just seemed like my prayers were going so far and falling back to the ground. Again I cried to God, "God, where are you?" He said, "I've been here since six o' clock. Where have you been?" Then, I realized what was happening. I repented and knelt before God in true brokeness. It became clear to me why God did not reveal the length of this fast. He showed me that after all this time the fast was only beginning. In other words, it took the first six days to show me where I really was in attitude and obedience toward Him. It was obvious I needed discipline. It took another six days, a total of twelve days, for God to break me completely and release me from the fast. During this time, I did not always set the alarm clock and God was faithful to help me get up. After having made a true commitment to obey Him, He even used birds chirping outside the window to get my attention to get me up. God is always faithful to prove Himself after we are obedient to Him.

CHAPTER 12

The way up- is down

by Larry Fannin

What are your needs? What are your expectations? Someone said, "He that expects nothing shall not be disappointed." A good friend of mine, Evangelist Steve Sampson, once said, "Our expectations put a demand upon God." Our expectations are very low because we are trying to meet our needs in our own abilities. We don't know how to seek God for the answers we need.

God's way is not like our ways, but His way is the best and only way. If you want to be a success in God and make it to the top, I have some exciting news for you... ***The way up in God begins by going down!***

How can I go up if I'm going down? Good question, let me try to explain.

Matthew 6:16-18 (NKJV) "Moreover, when you fast, do not be like the hypocrites, with a sad countenance. For they may appear to men to be fasting. Assuredly, I say to you, they have their reward. But you, when you fast, anoint your head and wash your face, so that you do not appear to men to be fasting, but to your Father who is in the secret place; and your Father who sees in secret will reward you openly."

Without the proper motive for fasting to seek the Lord all you will get is skinny! The Lord is *more* interested in the way you are seeking Him than the *why*. God looks beyond our outward forms and our proper religious words and sees deep into our hearts. The purpose of fasting is to bring us to the place of repentance, self-humbling and mourning.

We are afflicting our flesh, denying our soulish desires to draw near to the Lord. We need to do this so we can line up with God's will, not get God to line up with our will. You see, God does not need to fast, but we do, fasting is for us! Fasting is one of the ways of God given to us that we might seek Him, and *find Him!*

Consider these Scriptures:
IIChronicles 7:14 (NKJV) "***If my people*** who are called by my name will *humble themselves*, and *pray* and *seek my face*, and *turn from their wicked ways*, *then* I will *hear* from heaven, and will *forgive* their sin and *heal* their land."

Isaiah 58:3 (NKJV) "...why have we *afflicted our souls*, and you take no notice?"

Psalm 35:13b. (NKJV) "...My clothing was sackcloth, *I humbled myself* with fasting..."

Psalm 69:10a. (NKJV) "When I wept and *chastened my soul* with fasting."

Matthew 5:4 (NKJV) "Blessed are those who *mourn*, for they shall be comforted."

II Corinthians 7:10 (NKJV) "For Godly *sorrow* produces *repentance* leading to salvation..."

From these Scriptures we see that fasting is one means that we may use to bring our soul and our flesh into submission to the Lord.

Five Steps Down

We will see from *James Chapter 4* that there are five steps down.

Step 1: James 4:6-10 (NKJV) "But He gives more grace, therefore He says: "God resists the proud, but gives grace to the humble.Therefore, submit to God. Resist the devil and he will flee from you. Cleanse your hands, you sinners; and purify your hearts, you double-minded. Lament and *mourn* and weep! Let your laughter be turned to *mourning* and joy to gloom. *Humble yourselves* in the sight of the Lord, and He will lift you up."

Our number one enemy is not the devil! It's *pride!* Pride is self-exaltation, self-sufficiency, an attitude of "I can do it, I don't need anyone not even God." Pride was the devil's downfall in the beginning when he said his five "I wills."

Isaiah 14:12-15 (NKJV) "How art thou fallen from heaven, O Lucifer, son of the morning! How you are cut down to the ground, You who weakened the nations! For you have said in your heart: '*I will* ascend into heaven, *I will* exalt my throne above the stars of God; *I will* also sit on the mount of the congregation on the farthest sides of the north; *I will* ascend above the heights of the clouds, *I will* be like the Most High.' Yet you shall be brought down to Sheol, to the lowest depths of the Pit."

The hardest lesson we will ever learn is that we *can not* do it ourselves. It is also the easiest one to forget! God hates pride and rebellion. Many are under God's divine resistance and will stay there until they stop fighting God, turn and go His way.

When we turn, God gives us *grace.* Grace is God's favor, but also it is God's power and ability to do it. God's grace is made perfect in our weakness. We need His grace to stand, walk, believe and for forgiveness of our sin.

Let's compare Lucifer's five *"I wills"* with our Lord Jesus in *His Five Steps Down.*

Philippians 2:5-11 (NKJV) "Let this mind be in you which was also in Christ Jesus, who being in the form of God, did not consider it robbery to be equal with God, but made Himself of no reputation, taking the form of a servant, and coming in the likeness of men. And being found in appearance as a man, He humbled himself and became obedient to the point of death, even the death on a cross. Therefore God also has highly exalted Him and given Him the name which is above every name, that at the name of Jesus every knee should bow, of those in heaven, and of those on earth, and that every tongue should confess that Jesus Christ is Lord, to the glory of God the Father."

First (verses 5-7)
His attitude of mind was Godly. He knew who he was and His place with God. Not in a proud or boastful way but in a submissive, loving relationship. We should know who we are in Christ and be at peace with ourselves. There is something good in us, but only by His grace and to His glory.

Second (verse 7)
He became a bondservant (slave). This is the relationship of choosing to be a slave of love for life. We choose whose slave we are going to be; Ourselves, the world's, the devil's, or God's. In Old Testament times slaves were given the choice of freedom. They could go free and live their own life. But if a slave loved his master and wished to stay with him to serve him for the rest of his life,

then the master would pierce his ear, nailing it to his door. From that time on he was a "slave because of love" by his own choice.

Third (verse 8)
"He humbled himself and became obedient even to the point of death." Obedience is something we *learn.*

Hebrews 5:8 (NKJV) "Though He was a Son, yet He learned obedience by the things which He suffered."

Many of us only obey when it's convenient and when it doesn't cost us anything. But what our Lord Jesus did was choose to obey even unto death. We need that type of *radical obedience,* no matter what comes; temptations, trials, tests, disappointments, even if it means death, **"I will obey Him."** Our lives should be a daily walk of instant unquestionable obedience to God's Word and will without excuses. We don't achieve this kind of obedience overnight, it takes training through experience of life learning how to walk in God's will.

Fourth (verse 9)
The cross is the place of death, not a piece of jewelry that we hang around our neck or on our wall. Once we choose to obey, then comes the cross. What is the cross? Well, it's not your husband, your wife, your boss, your children or even your pastor! No, the cross is not a circumstance or people, the cross is for you to die on, it's for the death of that old selfish nature through a daily choosing to obey.

Luke 9:23-26 (NKJV) "Then He said to them all, "If anyone desires to come after Me, let him *deny* *himself,* and take up his cross daily, and follow Me. For whoever desires to save his life will lose it, but whoever loses his life for My sake will save it. For what advantages is it to man if he gains the whole world, and is himself destroyed or lost? For whoever is ashamed of Me and My words, of him the Son of Man will be ashamed when He comes in His glory, and in His Father's, and of the holy angels."

The outward circumstances only reveal like a mirror what is in us. The purpose of the cross is to seperate through death my selfish desires from God's desires. I must daily *choose* to submit my will to God's will. This is what it means to take up your cross and follow Jesus daily.

Fifth (verses 9-11)
Then God is exalted in us and through us! We are given His name, (represents His character), and we are given His authority to rule and reign in the midst of our enemies. Most of all, God the Father is glorified in the Son through our lives that causes others to confess that Jesus Christ is Lord! Just as Jesus was exalted, given a name and brought glory to God the Father!

Step 2: James 4:7 (NKJV) "Therefore submit to God. Resist the devil and he will flee from you."

Someone once said that when a Christian is dressed in the Armor of God, the devil doesn't know you from Christ Himself! I would love to see the devil run in terror from me more often. Trouble is, I spend a lot of time running from him. But, I find that when I am submitted to God's known will, I have great confidence and no fear of the devil. The devil will do everything he can to keep us from submitting to God's will because he knows when we are in submission to God and are abiding under God's covering, we become a threat to his kingdom. Submission means to recognize our place under God's authority and yield our will to God's perfect will. We only have authority when we are under God's authority. *All* authority is delegated from *the* supreme authority. What we need is to *stop* resisting God's will, and *start* resisting the devil by submitting to God's will. What God speaks we agree with and also speak the same, "It is written," what we see the Father doing is what we do. When we take authority over demons, Satan or spiritual forces, we must already be in submission to the one who has been given all authority in Heaven and on the earth, the Lord Jesus Christ. Then nothing is impossible to him that will believe and act within the reality of God's revealed will.

Step 3: James 4:8 (NKJV) "Draw near to God and He will draw near to you. Cleanse your hands, you sinners; and purify your hearts, you double-minded."

"Time to eat. Wash your hands." I can still hear my mother calling us to eat. We didn't eat her food with dirty hands. We don't receive from God with dirty hands either. To draw near to God, which begins on our part, is to come close to a Holy God who can't stand sin. He loves the sinner but hates the sin. God requires we wash our hands through repentance. This is the deed we have done or not done that we all know didn't please God. Purify your hearts from all wrong motives and those unnoticed attitudes that can creep in, like bitterness, jealousy, lust and disobedience. We need to stop being double-minded, having two opinions, about serving the Lord. Don't be wishy-washy, lukewarm or indecisive about it any more. If God be God then serve Him. Make that a once and for all commitment.

A high wire artist was going to ride a bike across Niagara Falls. He had a great reputation. He was the best on a wire, the best of the best at his art. He asked a bystander if he believed that he could ride his bike across the wire. The bystander said, "Sure, you can do it!" The performer then said, "Get on!" If we really believed all the nice religious talk that comes out of our mouths at church, then we will walk it. Get on with the Lord Jesus. Stop trying to have the best of both the world and its *pleasures* and the kingdom and its *treasures.* Get *right,* stay *right* and live *right* then life will go *right* for you and you will feel *right!*

Step 4: James 4:9 (NKJV) "Lament and mourn and weep! Let your laughter be turned to mourning and joy to gloom."

We can take sin so lightly sometimes. We are masters of justifying ourselves and at making excuses for our sin. True brokenness for our sin is what God requires, not being sorry I got caught, but truly sorry for my sin. All sin is against God Himself and grieves the Holy Spirit. When we see ourselves for what we really are in the light of God's holiness, then we will say, "Woe is me for I am a man of unclean lips." Only then can God's grace lift us up, cleanse us and bring us into the courts of the King! No more hidden sin! No more secret faults! What a feeling! Clean! Whole! Free! Living in His presence with peace, joy and righteousness in heart. Read ***Psalm 51*** and ***Psalm***

32. Make them your prayer as David did. Right now, really come clean before the Lord. You will be glad that you did.

Step 5: James 4:10 (NKJV) "Humble yourselves in the sight of the Lord and He will lift you up."

If we humble ourselves we will not be humiliated! There is a big difference! What does it mean to be humble?

1. Humility is a right attitude of dependence upon God, acknowledging that *We need Him.*
2. Humility is a thankful heart for His grace that saves us, keeps us and keeps on keeping us.
3. Humility is an attitude of a servant willing to serve in whatever capacity God needs us.
4. Humility is the freedom from the need of recognition from man. We only need to know we are pleasing the Father.
5. Humility is God's requirement for promotion, for the ***way up in God is first down.***

CHAPTER 13

Blind spots revealed through fasting

In April 1986, while spending time before the Lord, God led me to read the book of ***Philippians.*** In the first chapter, He took me to verses ***20-21 (NIV):***

"I will eagerly expect and hope that I will in no way be ashamed, but will have sufficient courage so that now as always Christ will be exalted in my body, whether by life or by death. For to me, to live is Christ and to die is gain."

From this scripture, I received a deep desire to be like Paul. I saw his total commitment to Christ and his willingness to die for Him. But I saw that in my flesh there was no good thing. This caused me to seek God and draw closer to Him so I could hear Him.

As I sought God wholeheartedly, He led me to fast. Not knowing how many days to fast, I pledged to go as long as He wanted me to. I cried out to God asking Him to search me and try my heart to see if there was anything in me not pleasing to Him. I did not know of any sin or anything that was in me, but I yearned so much to have a cleansing and a total commitment like that of Paul. I kept asking God to reveal any blind spots that might be hidden from me. God revealed three areas of my life during a ten-day fast.

The ***first area*** that God showed me was that I allowed myself to limit my vision and be satisified with my ministry in our local church. God was calling me to a deeper relationship in order for me not to fear, but to reach out to the multitudes and be used by God in ways

I never thought possible. He wanted me to take off the limits so He could use me in a bigger way to increase my vision and enlarge my heart. For me to stop thinking small and have a deeper relationship with Him, there would be a cost; more of Him and less of me. God wanted me to enter into a crucified life and give back to Him my all. I had to repent of my lack of commitment and seeing things in my small way rather than God's vast way.

The ***second area*** He revealed was my participation in the works of the flesh. I did not see what I was doing until one night God gave me a dream. In the dream, I saw a lady from our chruch in trouble with two policemen. They were trying to take her to jail. She was crying out and calling me, saying "Sun, Sun, please come and help me. I don't want to go to jail. Don't let them take me. Please help me." When I saw her crying for help, I ran to the policemen and asked them not to take her and they said, "We must." I realized my helplessness. I looked around and asked the people what I could do to help her. These people told me to follow her and to see the "big boss" to get help.

I entered a building. It was the most beautiful, spotless, clean building I could ever remember seeing. As I entered a particular room, the Big Boss was sitting at the desk. He showed great love and compassion in his eyes. I sat by his desk and asked this Big Boss to please help my friend. I was crying with a desperate heart, begging him to help her. Then, he looked at me with such compassion and said, "Look at yourself." As I looked at myself, I saw filthy clothes. My body was covered with dirt because I had worked hard and fallen down many times getting there. As I had been crying, I saw the dirty tears dripping from my face. I said, "Oh, I'm so dirty and filthy." Then he said, "Go wash yourself. Clean up and then return and place your petition."

I saw a man standing beside me who took me to a fountain that was flowing. He showed me the soap and towels to use. After I was cleaned up, I returned and placed my petition with the Big Boss. Then, I woke up.

I realized that what God showed me was my spiritual condition and how displeasing I was to Him.

Revelation 2:2-5 (NIV) "I know your deeds, your hard work and your perseverance. I know that you cannot tolerate wicked men, that you have tested those who claim to be apostles but are not and have found them false. You have persevered and have endured hardships for my name, and have not grown weary. Yet, I hold this against you: You have forsaken your first love. Remember the height from which you have fallen! Repent and do the things you did at first."

God opened my eyes and He taught me the true meaning of these Scriptures. I was amazed to see how all my effort in helping people was so displeasing to God. My efforts were as filthy rags. God cares more about the condition of the heart rather than the work we do in the ministry. We can easily get into our own fleshly works instead of taking time to seek His face, love and worship Him. God wanted me to have the personal relationship with Him. However, in the course of all my 'duties', I left my first love. I became so involved with duties that often I would get ahead of Him. At times, He wanted me to pray for the needs of others and instead, I was trying to meet those needs myself. I was working so hard, I was worn out and was not fulfilling my true ministry as an intercessor. I always felt that what God had done for my life was so great, I could never thank Him or do enough for Him. Being busy in the church, visiting and doing things for His people I thought was pleasing to God. I felt God was showing me all these things were good, but I needed to go back to my first love, seek Him and depend on Him to show me what direction to take and how to minister to His people. *He wanted me not to be their God,* but teach them how to go directly to Him. After God had shown me these things, I repented of my fleshly work and I felt so clean and refreshed.

A ***third area*** He showed me was that I needed to repent of pride and self-righteousness. On the sixth day of the fast, we were having a guest Evangelist in our church. When I went to church, I felt good and very refreshed. I felt there was nothing in my life to stop me from growing in the Lord and enjoying what God had given me and done for me. I was surprised to learn that there was a deep sin settled in my subconscious that God was about to root out. Being overzealous in the meeting, I stepped out and did something I should not have done. I felt strongly that God wanted me to minister to a few needs in people's lives. Many people responded to my call, and I prayed for them before the speaker came up to minister to us. I sat down and felt very uncomfortable. I felt very nervous and that something was wrong, but I did not know what it was.

We had a good meeting and I went home. However, I could not sleep because I was very restless. Without any doubt, I knew something was wrong but I could not put my finger on it.

The next day, my husband, Larry (who is the pastor) and I had a chance to sit down and talk. I had had uneasy feelings about last night so I was nervous and defensive before he could say anything to me. In the past, we had made a commitment that if either one of us did anything which was not right, then we would help each other correct it. Very lovingly and gently, Larry began to tell me that to get up and minister to the people before the speaker had a chance to was wrong. We had prayed and fasted for the speaker to hear from God. We were to trust God to use him to minister to the needs of the body. He assured me he knew I had heard God, but I missed the timing of the Lord. Before he could say anymore, I got angry and said, "That is it! I'm not going to do anything anymore." I stomped to the bedroom and flopped on the bed and started sobbing uncontrollably.

Larry came in and asked me what was wrong. I told him how clean I had felt after six days of fasting, only drinking water, and all God had done in my heart. I said, "Now, you're telling me I missed God when I am feeling so confident in the Lord. How can I trust myself to hear God any more?" He assured me I had not missed God, I had just missed His timing. However, I did not want to hear or receive my husband's comfort, so I pulled the blankets over me and cried even harder.

I was speaking out of my mouth, saying I cannot trust myself anymore after what I went through on this fast; but, deep inside my heart, I was afraid of what *people* were thinking and what the *Evangelist* was thinking of me.

Because of these meetings, we had a lot of guests from outside our church. I thought: "Here I am a pastor's wife; what are these people thinking?" I was so embarrassed and angry at myself for what I had done. This went on throughout the next day. I was so miserable; not wanting to talk or see anybody, just wanting to cover myself with the blankets and stay in bed.

When I fell asleep that night, God gave me this dream: In the dream, I went to the store and I saw a couple from our church. I did not want them to see me, so I hid. They saw me and asked me if I was okay. I did not speak honestly to them and told them I was fine. Then, the scene changed. I had a rope connected to a car that was running out of control. I tried to stop it with this rope, but I could not. I saw a bridge and the car fell off the bridge into the water. The car followed my leading so much easier in the water regardless of how I handled the rope. Then I woke up.

God interpreted this as the outrageous anger inside of me as a result of my pride. The car represented me and the water represented the Holy Spirit. I did not want to acknowledge it, but I had to admit it and let go of the anger. I kept hearing a still small voice inside me saying, "Your pride, your pride, yield to the Holy Spirit." I was still fighting with my flesh, and I kept trying to justify myself to God, arguing it was not my pride. I was disappointed with myself for messing up after all I had been through during this time of fasting and repentance. But I still kept hearing the small voice, "It's your pride, deal with it because it is hindering your spiritual growth."

I was angry with myself and was crying out to God saying, "I want to be close to You. I thought I was okay since I dealt with what You had shown me during this fast. Now, I am not sure. I want to be in Your perfect will, desiring so much to have a total commitment like Paul. Lord, I don't want to eat or drink anything until I receive perfect peace and comfort in my heart."

After getting up, I was afraid someone might come to see me. To avoid the possibility of seeing someone, I went shopping until mid-afternoon. I still did not escape because, when I returned home, there was a couple from our church waiting to see me. Not knowing what I had been going through for the past two days, they said the Lord laid on their hearts to come and see me. They asked me if I was okay. I lied, "Yes, I'm fine." They asked me again, "Is there something wrong? Your face shows us that there is." I said, "It is something personal and I have been crying; that is why my face is swollen. But, I'm okay, I'm fine."

"Are you fasting?", they asked.

After they found out how many days I had been fasting and that for two days I had not eaten or had anything to drink, the women (one being a Registered Nurse) told me how much I was hurting my body and to stop.

I started crying and told them everything that had been going on in my heart, "The more I tried to get close to God, the more I saw ugliness in me. For all God had done for me, all I ever wanted was to love and serve Him with a pure heart before Him. To be like Paul, whether I die or live, all I want is to see the Glory of God manifested in my life. Whatever it takes to get there I'm determined to pay the price. If it takes a forty or even a hundred-day fast to break every sin in my life, I will do it."

After listening to me they said, "Sun, one thing we want you to know is that *no matter how many days you fast, you can not twist God's arm.* You can not be perfect or pure over night. If you made a mistake during this fast, don't think you'll never make another one." They ministered to me in a beautiful way; calmed me down and prayed for me. Finally, I gave up and yielded myself to the Holy Spirit to take control over my life.

After they left, I sought God's mercy and forgiveness which He freely granted. As a loving Father, God is faithful to instruct His beloved children when he sees them turn to the left or to the right of the perfect plan He has personally designed for them.

I praise God for the breakthrough that came and the victory I received in my life as I yielded to the transforming work of the Holy Spirit. It took a total of ten days for God to do what He wanted to do in me, and I was truly thankful for His faithfulness to honor my request and show me the blind spots that were displeasing to Him even though, at the time, I did not realize what I was asking or what the cost would be. I praise God for His longsuffering with me.

CHAPTER 14

My first thirty day fast

After my ten days of fasting, the Lord gave me a burden for the Koreans and the Americans in the local area to unite for a time of prayer and fasting. He impressed upon my heart to pray for one hundred days. During this period of time in May of 1986, I met a woman Evangelist who was the American representative to the Korean Dr. Jashil Choi's "Fasting-Prayer Mountain" in Korea. (This is a mountain where Christians meet to fast and pray.) Immediately, she caught my attention. I clung to her every word as she shared her experiences with Dr. Jashil Choi.

Dr. Choi is the mother-in-law of the highly recognized pastor of the Yoido Full Gospel Church in Seoul, Korea, Dr. Paul Yonggi Cho. The current membership of this church is well over 500,000.

Besides her ministry at "Fasting-Prayer Mountain", Dr. Choi has ministered all over the world. She was also the Korean representative to a national meeting concerning prayer in America conducted by President Reagan. The Evangelist promised me Dr. Choi would be able to speak at our church the following September. Words could not describe my excitement and joy. I would not know how anyone could bring Korean and Americans together better than Dr. Choi. The thought of Dr. Choi coming to Greenfield, Indiana was like a dream!

During the month of June, 1986, I began a thirty-day fast with three goals in mind. The *first* goal was to write a book of my life story in English. The *second* goal was to attain more of the power of God in my personal walk and ministry. The *third* was the burning desire within my heart for revival in our church and among the Koreans in the local vicinity and revival in America.

I could not humanly comprehend a 30-day fast, drinking only water, but the assurance in my heart told me to be obedient. I knew with each passing day I would grow in God's grace and power. On the third day of the fast, God gave me a woman to help me write the book. I was amazed at how everything was working out so quickly and beautifully. God kept His promise by endowing His supernatural strength to me so I could continue living my normal lifestyle. My book "***The Bad Luck Baby***" was written in those thirty days.

After the fast, as the Evangelist promised, Dr. Choi arrived in September for three nights of speaking engagements to both Koreans and Americans. To be a part of this unity and revival was such a blessing. God truly answered my prayers in bringing the local Koreans and Americans together in prayer and worship in perfect love and unity. God opened doors that no man could shut.

God also granted my request for the anointing and power of God in my life and ministry. After thirty days of fasting, I felt the power of God would manifest mightly, but this did not happen. I did not *see* too much difference in my ministry. In my disappointment, I asked God, "Why? Was I expecting too much? Lord, why are these things not happening?" As I cried out to the Lord, He gave me this word.

"As you walk faithfully unto me and practice daily, denying yourself, taking up your cross and following Me, then it will come."

So, I had to daily practice dying to self and following Him and then He would fulfill these desires. Since that time, I have not questioned the Lord about this area of my life. I had released and was totally at rest in Him.

About a year after I had received that word from God, I was ministering in Ohio. God spoke to me that this would be a miracle service. It happened! A great miracle service manifested. After the meeting was over I had to pinch myself to make sure it was real! I knew it would come someday, as He had promised. I continued to be faithful to Him; but when I experienced it, it was truly exciting to see, God proved He is not a liar.

Numbers 23:19 (NIV) "God is not a man, that he should lie, not a son of man, that he should change his mind. Does he speak and then not act? Does he promise and not fulfill?"

Praise God for His faithfulness and goodness toward us.

CHAPTER 15

Revelation of New Beginning through fasting

In the beginning of 1988, both in my own personal life and in our church body, we were experiencing many spiritual battles. To keep from becoming discouraged, I had to discipline myself through fasting to maintain a better attitude. Many times I fasted to walk in victory from circumstances. Through fasting, I experienced many miracles and saw how God moved so faithfully in my life and in the church.

By mid-summer, I felt I had worked so hard doing spiritual battle that when everything seemed okay, I just wanted to take it easy for awhile. One morning, I got up and God impressed on my heart a fast. I did not know the reason why I needed to fast. The only reason I could think of was for the meetings that soon would be taking place. Right away, I refused to believe that it was from God. I found excuses by saying I had done enough fasting for the year. I did not want to get into a religious work or in bondage. I did not want to believe this request was from God. I felt it was just my flesh, so I rebelled against the word I had received. I continued to rebel for three weeks until I became so miserable I said, "Okay, Lord, if you want me to fast, I will." This was another time God did not show me how many days to fast. However, I was desperate enough that I was willing to go on as long as God wanted me to. I repented for my rebellion and disobedience toward God, but on the fifth day God still had not released me from this fast. I had no clear understanding from God why this fast was to continue, unless I was to spend time with Him. I had meetings scheduled in the Buffalo area in New York. The day after arriving in New York (which was the sixth day of my fast) I started the first meeting and God moved greatly in this meeting. I was so excited as it was my first trip to New York and my first meeting there. I was anxious to see what would happen in the future meetings and see how God was going to bless the people. The seventh day of my fast was a Sunday. I thought God would release me from the fast, but He did not do so. So I accepted whatever God had planned for me to do. It had to be good!

On Monday, the eighth day of my fast, we had a meeting in the evening. I saw how God moved miraculously healing people and breaking many bondages in their lives. I had seen God move mightily before, but not like this! There were varicose veins disappeared before our eyes, bunions disappeared and many other healing occured. Since this was a new experience for me, I was very excited. We greatly rejoiced in the Lord for what He had done that night during our meeting.

The next day, God released me from the fast of only drinking water to a partial fast of eating only fruit. I stayed in New York for a total of eight days and had a total of eight glorious meetings.

One night during this time in New York, I had a dream: In the dream, I saw a book which contained my testimony and teachings of how to fast. The book gave all of the needed information. I was passing it out to the people. This indicated to me that someday I was to have a book printed on prayer and fasting.

Also during this time in New York, God gave me a vision of a three-day prayer and fasting gathering. God directed me to go to the larger cities and bring people from every corner to fast and pray. This would pull down strongholds in their lives, homes, churches, cities, and our nation. God showed me as they came from all areas they would receive a spark in their hearts and learn how to stand in the gap through fasting and prayer. With this spark, these people would return to their homes and churches and, by standing in the gap, eventually would cause a flame of revival to break out in the nation.

He showed me that in order for me to see this happen, I needed to practice fasting and prayer faithfully in my own life. I also needed to have a three-day prayer and fasting gathering in our own local church and teach them. After my church fully understood the benefits of fasting and prayer, then He wanted me to go to the larger cities and present three-day prayer and fasting gatherings.

I left New York with great excitement in my heart. I was overjoyed with the new vision in the ministry and by what God had done. He had honored my fast! On the way home, I mentioned to my traveling companion about the number eight that seems to be related to many of the things happening lately. For example, we stayed in New York eight days, fasted eight days, and eight meetings (I even continued a partial fast for eight days). The most interesting thing of all that God had me start fasting on 8-8-88. We prayed and asked God to reveal to us what this means.

The next morning after arriving home, I woke up with a question in my mind. I was still asking God to please show me what this meant, if there was anything I needed to know. Then the Lord spoke to my heart the meaning of the number eight. Eight means new beginning! As soon as I heard this I jumped up out of bed with great excitement and started praising God. I realized that this was another turning point in my life and a new beginning in the ministry for the nation.

I obeyed the word and the vision God gave me by personal fastings and by having a three-day prayer and fasting gathering in our church. Until this time, I only taught the church about it, but we had not come together to fast and pray as a body. Beautiful results of this fasting were seen as heaviness and hindrances to receiving God's blessings were broken. Our church was never the same! After this, God laid it on my heart to have the first prayer and fasting gathering in Indianapolis, Indiana. I have to say I am not an administrator; nor am I a very organized person. When God showed me about this gathering, I had no idea how to structure such a meeting. I had only gone to scheduled services where all I had to do was speak. Now, I had to start at the beginning and I did not know how to organize a seminar. However, God took me step by step showing me how to plan every detail.

The first meeting was in Indianapolis during April of 1989. The second meeting was held in Evansville, Indiana, during August, 1989. Both gatherings were great! God truly showed Himself to us and honored those who humbled themselves to fast and pray. They went home with great joy and victory in their lives.

At the first gathering in Indianapolis, God dealt with me about having a deeper commitment. It was at this time that He said He would use me all over the nation.

The second gathering in Evansville was an honor from God for the commitment I had made in April, and the faithfulness I had before Him. He had shown Himself to me in a way I had never dreamed. In the first evening meeting in Evansville, we had great blessing from a ministry called "The Little Sisters." They had an unexpected surprise for me. God put on their hearts to honor this unworthy servant by making a very special banner. From morning until night for many days "The Little Sisters" worked and prayed together making the banner.

In February, 1990, God helped me and provided the right people to put this book together. He has also honored me by allowing me to have four, three-day prayer and fasting gatherings during 1990. This is twice the number of gatherings which I held in 1989. It is very exciting to see God fulfill His word.

CHAPTER 16

The power of the lie

by Larry Fannin

Isaiah 58:8 (NKJV) "Then your *light* shall break forth like the morning. Your healing shall spring forth speedily, and your righteousness shall go before you; the glory of the Lord shall be your rear guard."

Another benefit of fasting and prayer is the light of truth shining into our life through the Spirit of Truth the Holy Spirit.

Before we were born again by the Holy Spirit, we walked in darkness, our hearts and minds were darkened by sin and the prince of darkness.

Colossians 1:13-14 (NKJV) "He has delivered us from the power of darkness and translated us into the Kingdom of the Son of His love, in whom we have redemption through His blood, the forgiveness of sins."

The great conflict of the ages rages in the world, and we are caught up in the middle of it. The prize is the souls of men. It's the conflict between the Kingdom of Light, God's truth, and the Kingdom of Darkness, Satan's deception. Satan's goal is to *blind* our minds that he may *bind* our will so that we can not serve the Lord as we desire.

II Corinthians 4:4 (NKJV) "Whose minds the god of this age has blinded, who do not believe, lest the *light* of the gospel of the glory of Christ, who is the image of God, should shine on them."

Even after we are born again and transferred into the Kingdom of Light, there still remains *in us* areas of darkness that blind and bind us. We all have areas with which we struggle and fail to understand why we aren't gaining any victory. Satan is a master deceiver who has centuries of practice. Without the Holy Spirit we are no match for him.

If you find yourself still struggling with the same problems of doubt, unbelief, fear, worry or some sin over which you can't keep victory; I have good news for you. There is a way provided for us to be free. We can have victory and maintain the victory. We just need to know how to walk in the Light so that the darkness will be exposed. When we walk into a dark room and turn on the light the darkness is gone. Light is greater than darkness; it doesn't matter how small the light, it always dispels darkness. A small match burning in a darkened room gives light by which to walk. Through fasting and prayer, we can allow the Holy Spirit to shine the light of Truth in us and illuminate the dark areas of our lives. When we come to the knowledge of the Truth, it will set us free from the lies of the devil. We need to learn how to walk in the Light and allow the Light to grow in us until we are full of the Light and become Lights that shine in the dark world.

John 8:44 (NKJV) "You are of your father the devil, and the desires of your father you want to do. He was a murderer from the beginning, and does not stand in the truth, because there is no truth in him. When he speaks a lie, he speaks from his own resources, *for he is a liar and the father of it."*

In this passage of scripture we see the power of the lie. The Pharisees were blind to the truth and could not see the truth standing before them and speaking with them. The power of the lie is that those who believe it are blinded by it and truth to them looks like darkness. Truth is lie to them and lie is truth. They were deceived and didn't know it. The father of lies had blinded them to the point they couldn't see it.

What we are today is the result of what we have accepted as truth in the past.

Proverbs 23:7 (NKJV) "For as a man thinks in his heart so is he."

Satan, as the master deceiver, has effectively planted his "lie seeds" into our minds. The lies have taken root and grown to produce *"blind spots"* in us.

Romans 1:25 (NKJV) "...who exchanged the truth of God for the lie, and worshiped and served the creature rather than the Creator, who is blessed forever. Amen."

We can come to the place that we *'exchange'* the truth of God for the lies of Satan. We need another exchange where we *'exchange'* the lie for the Truth through the Word of God illuminated by the Spirit of Truth.

Psalm 19:12 (NKJV) "Who can understand his errors? Cleanse me from secret faults."

Blind spots are areas in us that we don't see. We are blind to our own actions and weaknesses. Secret faults are blind spots, things we don't see; not only some secret sin that we are practicing and hiding from others. The power of the lie is we really don't see it! Others may see it and try to help us, but we don't see it. We need to see our need then we can be free from the blindness.

Psalm 139:23-24 (NKJV) "Search me O God, and know my heart; try me, and know my anxieties; And see if there is *any* wicked way in me, and lead me in the way everlasting."

As we allow the Lord to search us He will reveal our blind spots. This can be a very painful experience because it may require a painful trial to expose to us our blindness. King David had a heart after God, yet had a secret fault of which he was unaware. It was exposed when he sinned with Bathsheba. David didn't fall over night, the sin exposed this weakness. The Lord used David's failure to expose him in order to heal him. Our failures can be turned to our good by the Lord who exposes our sin and delivers us from Satan's lies.

James 1:14-15 (NKJV) "But each one is tempted when he is drawn away by his own desires and enticed. Then when desire has conceived, it gives birth to sin; and sin when it is full-grown, brings forth death."

We need to understand how Satan deceives us; how he plants his lie seed in us and causes blind spots. He attacks our minds with seed thoughts to deceive us and get us to believe his lie. *It is what is in us that defeats us.* The enemy must gain access to our minds through enticing us and continually tempting us until we accept the lie.

John 14:30 (KJV) "For the prince of this world cometh, and hath nothing in me."

Jesus was tempted, but there was nothing *(not a thing)* in Him that Satan could appeal to. Jesus had no sinful nature. We do! Even after we are born again and become new creatures, if we do not live in the Truth, the old sin nature, the carnal mind and the old man that is dead, can rise up again! It is much easier to get us into the Kingdom than it is to get the Kingdom into us!

The warfare begins in the mind. He who controls the minds of men controls the world. Satan is an expert at brainwashing. He begins at our birth and never stops. Through childhood bruises, hurts, wounds caused by rejection, he plants his lie seeds in us. The lie seeds grow, affecting our personalities and our emotional health. Through physical abuse, sexual abuse, neglect of the parents and the worst form of child abuse, verbal, he attacks us until we accept the lie. His lies destroy our self-image and feelings of self-worth. The lie hinders us from accepting God's love and becoming all that God had created us to be. God has given us many good gifts that will produce good works for His Kingdom, but Satan has polluted them and distorted the image of Christ in us that we can not be who we really are because of being bound to the false image of ourselves.

James 1:12 (NKJV) "Blessed is the man who endures temptation; for when he has been proved, he will receive the crown of life which the Lord has promised to those who love Him."

When we endure temptation and come through without sin, we are blessed. Trial and testing proves us. We are approved after we pass the test. Like testing metal for strength, putting it into the fire and testing it for hardness. When the metal is approved no weakness will be found in it. The firey trials test us and reveal areas of weakness in us that we may be healed and not sin. God wills healing and wholeness. Satan wills death and defeat.

James 1:13 (NKJV) "Let no one say when he is tempted, 'I am tempted by God'; for God cannot be tempted by evil, nor does He Himself tempt anyone."

God does not tempt us with evil or to do any evil. God isn't the one tempting you to rob a bank or to commit adultery. God allows the testing of our faith, but Satan is the 'tempter', the one who uses evil temptation to defeat us. All temptation to sin is from the devil, not God.

James 1:14 (NKJV) "But each one is tempted when he is drawn away by his own desires and enticed."

It is what is *in* us that defeats us. We are drawn away from the truth and enticed by our reaction to the temptations set before us. Satan set a trap and uses our weaknesses as bait. For some it is greed, the love of money. For others it is lust, sexual temptations, pride, an independent spirit, self-sufficiency, etc. He knows by our *reactions* which bait to use. When he finds one that works, he uses it to get our attention. It is just a matter of time until we take the bait. Just as certain lures will work on certain fish, and look like the real thing, so Satan knows by watching us and listening to us which temptation to set before us. As an expert fisherman knows how to work the lures to attract the fish, so Satan knows how to get our attention. Once we look to his bait, we're hooked.

James 1:15 (NKJV) "Then, when desire has conceived, it give birth to sin; and sin, when it is fullgrown, brings forth death."

The bait appeals to a desire in us. Satan's thought seeds appeal to the blind spots. When we take the bait, then the thought seed takes root *in us*, in our mind. It then conceives giving birth to sin. When we are tempted it's not sin until we don't stop and *resist it.* Then, as we *accept* the lie into our minds we are bound even before we commit any outward act.

Matthew 5:28 (NKJV) "But I say to you that whoever looks at a woman to lust for her has *already* committed adultery with her in his *heart.*"

Now, Satan has us. We are blinded, bound in that area of our minds and death is already working in us to destroy us. We have swallowed the bait and the hook is set, now Satan can control us and reel us in. We may fight it, but eventually he wears us out and we become tired, weak and we don't know why.

Hebrews 12:3b (NKJV) "...lest you become weary and discouraged in your souls."

Romans 8:5 (NKJV) "For those who live according to the flesh set their minds on the things of the flesh, but those who live according to the Spirit, the things of the Spirit."

Sin begins in the mind before it ever becomes an act. There is something in us (our soulish realm), a blind spot, a past wound, or personal weakness, that gives fertile ground for the thought seeds of temptation. The ground in our hearts needs to be weeded of all the blind spots (wounds in our soul), so that we can say as Jesus did, "He has nothing in me." ***Read John 14:30.***

It begins in the mind:

II Corinthians 11:3 (NKJV) "But I fear, lest somehow, as the serpent deceived Eve by his craftiness, so your minds might be corrupted from the simplicity that is in Christ."

Satan's strategy is deceptive and it has not changed since the beginning. It is amazing how easily we fall for his lies. We need to understand how deception works so that we can guard our minds. In Genesis, chapters two and three, we have the account of Adam and Eve. God had given them everything to enjoy except one tree. One would think if we had all we ever wanted, that we would be satisfied.

The forbidden fruit has tremendous drawing power. Just try telling your children, "No! Don't touch!" As soon as you turn your back, they go for it. Even when we understand the consequences for sin, we still do it.

Genesis 3:1 (NKJV) "Now the serpent was more cunning than any beast of the field which the Lord God had made. And he said to the woman, 'Has God indeed said, 'You shall not eat of every tree of the garden?"

The devil begins by getting our attention through thoughts to gain control of our minds. He does this by asking us a question. When we respond to his question, he has us thinking, he has our attention.

Genesis 3:2-3 (NKJV) "And the woman said to the serpent, 'We may eat the fruit of the trees of the garden; but of the fruit of the tree which is in the midst of the garden, God has said, 'You shall not eat it, nor shall you touch it, lest you die."

Eve must have already desired the forbidden fruit for her answer added to what God had commanded. She said, "We can't touch it." God didn't say that (see ***Genesis 2:16-17***), his command was to take care of the garden, but don't eat of this fruit. The question triggered something in her and started her thinking in the direction that the devil wanted her to go.

Jesus was tempted but he overcame by quoting, "It is written." When He was asked the question, he responded with the Truth of God's word, not with His own reasonings. He did not dialogue with Satan, He resisted him with the Truth. Jesus knew the Word well. He knew when it was changed by adding to or leaving out some of the Truth.

We are *tricked* into deceiving ourselves. "The Bible has a lot to say about *self-deception.*"

James 1:22 (NKJV) "But be doers of the word, and not hearers only, *deciving yourselves.*"

We only possess the truth that we live and practice. The deception is that we think we know more than we do. We are good at hearing sermons and good teachings. We are well read and have collected tapes and have an abundance of knowledge. The average person in our churches has heard much. The problem is we don't hear it as *the Word of God,* which calls for obedience. Some have become people who "know-it-all", but when life begins to fall apart, so do they! We will produce fruit of that knowledge if we really *know.* We are known by our fruit.

For example, if we hear the sermon is to be on *Prayer,* we click off in our minds, because we have heard so many good sermons on prayer. The same ones who have heard it all *do not pray!* If we could take a survey of all Christians and find out how many actually have a good regular prayer life, I think that we would be shocked at the results. The same is true for other principles we know like, Fasting, Tithing, Bible Study, and Submission.

The truth of God's word must be built into our lives until we stand on it as rock solid, unmovable and unshakable through any kind of circumstance.

I John 1:8 (NKJV) "If we say that we have no sin, *we deceive ourselves,* and the truth is not in us."

We are good at justifying ourselves, rationalizing our actions, covering up our faults and blaming others or circumstances to keep from taking personal responsibility for our sin. Until we confess our sins, God can not forgive and cleanse us from them.

Galatians 6:3 (NKJV) "For if anyone thinks himself to be something, when he is nothing, he deceives *himself.*"

King Saul lost his authority and blessing because he acted in disobedience. When he was confronted by the prophet Samuel, he did not acknowledge his sin but put the blame on others. When we are convicted by the Holy Spirit, the only response we have is immediate repentance. God will redeem our mistakes, but He will punish our willful disobedience.

I John 2:9-11 (NKJV) "He who says he is in the light, and hates his brother is in the darkness until now. He who loves his brother abides in the light, and there is *no cause* for stumbling in him. But he who hates his brother is in darkness and *walks in darkness,* and does not know where he is going, *because* the darkness had *blinded his* eyes."

Broken relationships, hurts, wounds that result in bitterness and resentment cause blindness. If we are not healed and if we do not forgive, then the result in us will be self-deception. I have known people who were consumed with hate and bitterness. They had lost their spiritual eyesight and now all they could see was the offense. They were open to even more severe deception, blinded by the darkness. They became sick in their bodies and aged beyond their years. When we tried to help them they would reject the Truth that would set them free and then they rejected us. What a great darkness! Walk in the light. Don't allow any darkness in you. Don't take one step into the darkness, always turn from it and run into the light. Live in the light.

Galatians 6:7-8 (NKJV) "Do not be deceived, God is not mocked; for whatever a man sows, that he will also reap. For he who sows to his flesh will of the flesh reap corruption, but he who sows to the Spirit will of the Spirit reap everlasting life."

To deny God's law of sowing and reaping is like defying the law of gravity by jumping off a tall building. It is a spiritual law that does not show any respect for persons. What we sow in time we will reap. Where we sow, to the flesh or to the Spirit will reproduce a crop accordingly. We know that negative sowing works by experience. But the truth that will set us free is that the positive side of this spiritual law works in the same way. We need to plant the good seed of the Word of God into the good soil of our hearts so that we will bear the good fruit of the good life from a *good* God.

How do we do it?

Determine to be a doer of the Word and not just a hearer. Take personal responsibility for any sin and confess it immediately. Walk in forgiveness towards others, bless them and pray for them.

Continually plant the seed of God's Word into your heart and mind. Make it your determined purpose to obey God and please Him in all that you do.

CHAPTER 17

The purpose and benefits of fasting

Fasting and prayer is special times during which we deny ourselves for the purpose of seeking God's will:

Joel 2:15 (KJV) "Blow the trumpet in Zion, *sanctify a fast,* call a solemn assembly."

To sanctify means:

1. To set apart for religious use; to consecrate.

2. To set apart as holy; to give up for purpose of devotion.

3. To make holy or free from sin; to purify.

4. Sanctification results in a right feeling before God; free from guilt.

In other words, *to sanctify a fast* means: "To set ourselves and our time apart to God for the purpose of drawing near to Him in a spirit of true repentance and dedication."

Before we can enter into ministry that is truly blessed and anointed by God, we must be willing to deny ourselves and take the time to seek God.

We have already named some of the benefits of fasting but I want to give you more in order to encourage you to receive *all* that God has for you. Also, with a clear understanding of the purpose for fasting, you will have the truth that will set you free.

1. To destroy the works of the enemy:

Read Esther 4.

Israel was in danger of being destroyed as a nation.

Esther called the people to fast for three days, eating and drinking nothing. The results were that God exposed the deception of Haman (the enemy) and Israel was saved. We are hearing much today about God calling the church to intercessory prayer for our nation. God always begins with His people when He is preparing to do something in the earth. America is at the crossroads of judgment and revival. The church needs desperately to seek God for mercy and revival.

II Chron. 7:14 (NIV) "*If my people*, who are called by my name, will humble themselves and pray and seek my face and turn from their wicked ways, then will I hear from heaven and will forgive their sin and will heal their land."

Just as the people of Israel turned to God, we the church in America need to turn to God in order that the demonic forces which are trying to destroy our nation may be defeated.

2. **To bring repentance that will turn God's judgment into revival: *Read Jonah 3.***
   The sins of Nineveh reached God's throne and He sent Jonah to warn them that they had forty days to repent or He would destroy them. After they fasted and prayed three days, and repented from their sins, God's judgment was stopped. This is a key for bringing repentance to the church and our nation, that will turn God's judgment into revival. ***(Read Joel 2:12-13)***

3. **To win over impossible circumstances:**
   Read II Chronicles 20.
   Israel was surrounded and outnumbered. They fasted and set themselves to seek God for help. God spoke divine revelation which exposed all the plans of the

enemy enabling them to win. God fought the battle for them as they obeyed, and marched out singing praise unto the Lord. It took several days to gather up the spoils of the enemy.

Many times we find ourselves facing impossible circumstances where we can't see any possible way out. But if we will set our hearts to seek the Lord through prayer and fasting, God does have the answer for us. For nothing is impossible with God if we are just willing and obedient. ***(Read Isaiah 1:19)***

4. **To receive revelation and bind the ruling strong man's spirit: *Read Daniel Chapters 9-10.***

   Daniel fasted and prayed twenty one days for his nation. He understood by reading the Word of God in the prophet Jeremiah that the time of captivity was over. He received revelation of spiritual warfare in the heavenlies. Then Gabriel, the angel, came to him and gave revelation concerning the will of God. Study Daniel's prayer to see that he prayed and confessed Israel's sin as his own. This is how he stood in the gap for them. As he did this the power of God was released to destroy the spiritual forces in the heavenlies. As we pray and fast God will show us we can win the war and we will see our nation turn to God.

   Ezekiel 22:30 (NKJV) "I looked for a man among them who would build up the wall and stand before me in the gap on behalf of the land so I would not have to destroy it, but I found none."

   God is seeking. Will we be one who is found willing to do His will?

5. **To receive power and anointing for ministry and power to overcome the tempter:**
Read Luke 4:1-18.
We receive powerful faith to resist the daily temptations that come to defeat us through fasting and prayer. When we fast we set our hearts and minds on spiritual things and lose our interest in the things of the world. One main purpose of fasting is we can *hear God and submit ourselves to His will.* Hidden sins that have caused an open door for Satan to afflict us are closed and through the blood they are washed away. We find help, mercy, and grace to do God's will as we come to the throne of Grace.

Jesus was led by the Holy Spirit to fast. There are times of self-discipline when we practice fasting to keep our flesh under submission to the Spirit.

We need to fast as Jesus fasted. Because after His fast He received the power to carry out His ministry. Jesus overcame every temptation to the flesh and defeated the devil through yielding to His father's will. ***Hebrews 4:15*** shows us that Jesus was tempted in all points, like we are *yet without sin.* Our will to sin can be broken and we can become yielded to the *Lord's* will through fasting and prayer. Our spirit will die without spiritual food. Fasting allows our spirit to eat and become strong in the Spirit realm.

Matthew 4:4 (NKJV) "Man shall not live by bread alone, but by every word that comes from the mouth of God."

6. **To receive a reward from God:**
Read Matthew 6:16-18.
God wants a pure motive for us to receive the reward. God judges hypocritical attitudes, but rewards the pure in heart openly so others will see and He will be glorified. God doesn't measure success like men do.

He looks upon our hearts and judges our motives, not our performance. He knows where we are and how much we can do. His grace is sufficient and He is patient as He sees our hearts and desires to learn His ways. ***Read II Samuel 12:13-23.*** Fasting will not change God's will, but it will give us the grace to accept it. Just as the baby born to David and Bathsheba died even though David fasted. David was able to accept God's will and go on. We must learn to allow God to form us as He wills. The reward of God is worth laying down all of our ways and letting Him have His ways.

CHAPTER 18

Questions commonly asked about fasting

What is the difference between Normal, Total and Partial (Denial) Fasts?

A Normal fast is nothing to eat and only water to drink. The dictionary defines it as "to abstain from food," and the Greek word defines it as "a religious abstainence from food." This is a Normal fast. The Word shows us that Jesus did a normal fast and that he was hungry after His fast. It did not say that He was thirsty ***(Luke 4:2).***

A Total fast is nothing to eat or drink. Esther did a total fast for three days ***(Esther 4:16).*** Longer than that may be harmful to your health.

A Partial (or Denial) fast can be done several ways. For example, fruit only, vegetables only, a light meal a day or liquid only such as diluted fruit juices. Daniel is an example of a partial fast. He fasted for 21 days not eating pleasant food ***(Daniel 10:2-3).*** A partial fast is not meant to be a weight loss diet. Be sure you examine your motives!

How long should I fast?

It does not matter how long you fast, or how you fast, even one meal a day, what counts is that it is done unto God. It is important to seek God first, and let Him show you how long and on what type of fast you should begin.

Who should not fast?

Some medical authorities tell us that those with the following condition should not fast: Diabetes, heart disease, liver and kidney disease. I do not recommend fasting in these situations. A *Partial fast* may be more suitable. Your faith level and what God tells you should make the difference. It is very important to seek God to see what He is speaking to your heart.

Can we take medicine when we are fasting?

You should check with your physician first before fasting. *Again, it is very important to seek God to see what He is speaking to your heart.*

Why is it necessasry to drink a lot of water?

It is very important to drink plenty of water. Distilled water or boiled water is best. Drink at least two quarts a day, and preferably more. You can never drink too much water. Water is a very healthy nutrient. We need the water to help the body rid itself of excess fat breakdown and waste products.

Can I drink coffee and tea?

The caffeine in coffee and tea stimulates your nervous system which counteracts the restful state in which you want your body during a fast. Caffeine also stimulates your appetite.

Can I exercise?

Yes! Fresh air and exercise will do your body good. Walking will actually give you energy and gives you time to talk to the Lord.

Should I take an enema?

During a prolonged fast it is good to take a water enema daily for the first three days and every three days thereafter. Don't be surprised at the coal black liquid substance that comes from your body. Obviously, this helps to clean the crude substance that has built up over the months and years in the lining of your colon.

Should children fast?

Yes! As long as they are willing and have a full understanding about fasting. ***(Read Esther 4)***

What do we need to do during a prolonged fast?

It is best to do only the necessary activities in order to conserve your strength and spend time with the Lord. This does not mean you have to stay home from work!

How do I begin a fast?

You can prepare for your fast by decreasing the amount and type of food you eat. It is best to discontinue eating meat and eat more easily digested food. However, I usually begin the fast when God tells me without preparation.

How do I end a fast?

As many days as you fasted, that is the amount of days you should take to come off it. For example, if you fasted fourteen days, allow fourteen days to gradually progress to a regular diet. Begin with liquids such as diluted fruit juice, broth, soft foods, vegetables and fruits. Stay away from meat. Meats should be added last. Begin with small amounts. *How you come off the fast is as important as how you fast.*

Can I fast from something other than food?

Yes! It depends on what the Lord puts on your heart. I have a friend who likes to watch football every Sunday. God dealt with him to spend time praying and reading the Word of God, so he fasted the watching of football games in order to spend time with the Lord.

Is it wrong to fast to lose weight?

Fasting with the purpose of losing weight is a "false fast." There are many people who fast purely for health reasons and for their figure. This is fine, but this is not to be confused with a spiritual fast.

Should I discontinue the fast if I accidently break my fast or fail by eating something?

If you give in and fail by eating something, don't let Satan deceive you. God will not condemn you. Just shake off the accusing words and keep going toward the goal you have set. You must remember, God rewards your heartfelt motivation to obey Him.

What do we do about well-meaning relatives and friends who try to discourage us?

People will often tell us we should not fast. They will say you will get sick or you are too skinny already and you look pale. My mom, when I began to fast, used to be terrified because in her mind she thought the more you eat the healthier you become. You must go with the burden of the Lord and He will give you strength to fulfill your fast.

Can God lay a fast on your heart without your knowing the purpose?

Isaiah 55:8 (NIV) "For my thoughts are not your thoughts, neither are your ways my ways, declares the Lord."

As we humble ourselves to fast in obedience to the leading of the Holy Spirit, we become more sensitive to hear God's voice. As we open and examine our hearts, He will reveal the blind spots and show us the purpose of the fast. There have been times when I have fasted, not knowing the purpose. However as I humbled myself before God, seeking Him for the purpose for the fast, He was faithful to show me the blind spots and also the purpose for the fast. At times, it is an aid for a time of intercessory prayer and spiritual warfare. You may or may not know, the purpose at the time. The important thing is to obey the leading of the Holy Spirit.

Can you fast for someone else?

Yes! *Esther 4.* Israel was in danger of being completely destroyed as a nation. Verse 16: Esther called the people to fast and pray for her so she could go to the King and save her nation. When the people of Israel heard the news, they fasted and prayed. God exposed the deceiver and God's people were saved.

Is it wrong to tell anyone about my fast, since the Bible shows us to fast in secret?

Matthew 6:16 shows us not to fast as the hypocrites fast. Jesus is telling us not to fast to show off or be pleasing to men. The Pharisee's fasted, but there was no real repentance or humbling before God. You can share with someone who will stand in the gap and in agreement with you for your fast. ***(Read Matthew 18:19)***

Can fasting deliver us from doubt and unbelief?

Matthew 17:20-21: Fasting reaches and obtains what prayer alone cannot. Fasting removes unbelief. As you humble yourself, and deny the flesh, allowing God to take control of your life through fasting, you will experience the power of God. When you experience the power of God, unbelief will disappear.

Epilogue

God's faithfulness and His mercy endure forever. In the summer of 1984, I went to Seoul, Korea and visited the Yoido Full Gospel Central Church. Dr. Paul Yonggi Cho is the pastor of this church which is the largest church in the world. I also visited Dr. Jashil Choi's (the mother-in-law of Dr. Paul Yonggi Cho) "Fasting-Prayer Mountain".

I saw Koreans come to Prayer Mountian by the thousands to fast and pray. Most of them stayed three days but some stayed for a period of forty days. I was amazed to see these Korean people humble themselves, deny their flesh, and seek God. As I now live in America, I cannot understand why Americans do not turn to God and humble themselves as the Koreans. I began to see that the Americans are so busy doing everything else that they don't set apart time for God. As a result, the anointing of the Holy Spirit is not released in their lives to bring forth the healings and miracles which they would like to see. I had never seen anything like this until I returned to Korea. Thousands of people were in the sanctuary calling upon God with desperation in their hearts. It was magnificent to see God's power being released. I saw a growth, the size of a fist, dissolved from someone's neck. I saw the lame walk and the blind open their eyes. People experienced freedom and joy as they worshipped and praised by totally surrendering themselves to the Holy Spirit.

They have four services daily. In each service, they pray for America to repent and to experience revival. Thousands of prayer requests come from America alone. The Koreans, in one voice, cry out for God to bless

America. On my first visit, I stayed three days and repented of my sins. Although I am a native born Korean, I became an American citizen. I had not been praying for the nation in which I was now living. I felt ashamed. I was focused on myself instead of having God's burden for America. I asked God to give me His burden for America as the Christians in Korea.

After three days of prayer and fasting, I had a new outlook on America and I could not wait to return to America and share this with our church. Little did I know that this was the beginning of my ministry for America.

After I returned from Korea, I started to apply more prayer and fasting in my own life. I learned through prayer and fasting that I could yield my will to the will of God. As my old carnal nature was crucified, I became more sensitive to the Holy Spirit. Having a stronger hunger for the Lord caused me to gain a closer relationship with Him.

In 1986, God burdened my heart to fast for thirty days. I had three goals in mind:

1. To write my life story (testimony) in English.
2. I wanted to obtain more of the anointing of God in my life and ministry.
3. I desired to see revival in our local church and in America.

My book ***"The Bad Luck Baby"*** was written and published. I have experienced the power of God in my life as never before, but I have not seen the revival in America, that I have such a burden for.

A few months after my thirty-day fast in September, 1986, Dr. Jashil Choi came to Indiana. While in Indiana, she held a three-day meeting in our local church. One night she stayed in our home and while there she opened her heart and shared her burden with me. She said, "I realized the burden you had for America. God used American missionaries to come to Korea to plant the Gospel seed. Now, Korea is blessed because of their faithfulness to God. The churches are growing rapidly and revival is seen in the land."

Then she continued saying, "Pride has entered into the Americans. They have left their first love because of riches and glory in their land. Now America is corrupt, full of sin, sexual perversion, drugs, and alcohol. America is taking God's blessings for granted. Because of the American missionaries, Korea has the blessings of God and we feel we owe it to America to pray for a revival in their land. My heart's desire is to teach and help Americans understand the power of prayer and fasting. As much as I want to travel to every corner of America, I am limited. First, I don't speak English well, and I am getting older. I don't know how much more I can do for America. However, I feel you can fulfill God's desire for America.

"I believe the reason I am here for your church is because God saw your tears and He heard your prayers for America. God sent me here for you so that I can impart the gift of prayer and fasting and the burden of God for this nation to you. Normally, it takes two or three years for me to go where I am invited. For me to be here in a small town and a small church, like yours, is only a work of God."

Dr. Choi prayed for me to go forward to do the ministry. I did not fully comprehend what was going on at the time or what I had to do to deal with this burden for America.

God began to open many doors for me to carry out this burden. In 1988, my first trip was to the Buffalo area in New York. I received a revelation to have a three-day prayer and fasting gatherings. I also had a revelation to write a book about prayer and fasting.

In 1989, I held my first prayer and fasting gathering in Indianapolis, Indiana. During this time, God wanted me to make a deeper commitment and follow through completely. God also enlarged my heart and increased within me, the burden for America.

There were not as many people as I would liked to have seen, but God warned me that a big crowd would not come to this type of meeting. The ones that came were hungry for God and His anointing. They had received much healing and deliverance in their lives during the meetings, and they were stirred up about having a revival in America. God used me to impart the burden for America to them. After the meetings I had great joy in my heart.

After the last night meeting of this prayer and fasting gathering, I had a dream. In the dream, I was floating in the Pacific Ocean. I saw myself peaceful, beautiful, and calm. I flowed with the water wherever it flowed. Then I saw a water slide before me. I got on the slide and tried to climb to the top. I put all my energy into this, but I could not reach the top. I became tired and worn out. I kept sliding backwards and eventually fell into the ocean. It was like falling into pitch darkness. I was terrified! Then I woke up. After the dream, I thought, what a contrast! The scene was beautiful and calm, but also a terrifying experience. I asked God for the interpretation of my dream. He showed me that the ocean represents a world wide ministry if I commit everything unto Him and try not to do it on my own. In the natural, to float in the water I have to totally let go of myself and relax. If I try to fight, stiffen in the water, I will drown instead of floating. God has called me to a world wide ministry, but the condition is to totally let go, not to look at circumstances or let the flesh control me. Trust the Lord with all my heart, and do whatever He desires to fulfill the ministry that can glorify Him.

The water slide represented security such as the natural things in my life that I put before God. The natural things could be my family, my ministry, money, people, or myself (pride). The fleshly things in my life, that I hold on to, would prevent the anointing of God to flow freely through me. Therefore, I would accomplish very little for the kingdom of God. A water slide has water on the surface, but not enough to control me. When I try to hang onto things of the flesh or try to do things of the flesh it causes the anointing to be very small in me because I am still in control. But when I let go of myself, the Holy Spirit can be in full control and I will have the full anointing of God. Therefore, I would accomplish much for the kingdom of God. It is as if God is warning me to stay off the water slide because holding onto the natural things of the world will eventually cause me to fail. He wants me to be a willing vessel so I can have peace and beauty in my life.

At the beginning of 1990, I wrote a book on prayer and fasting, spending much time and effort in preparing it for print. After much re-work, it is now ready for publication in 1991. The finances were slow coming in to publish it. In September, I made a trip to the Buffalo area of New York, to speak at several engagements. At that time my book was completely ready for publication but the finances were still short by $5,000. I had received $50 on Saturday, after speaking at a women's group, this was the first meeting after arriving in New

York. On Sunday I felt God saying, "Out of your need give it all." I DID!

During this trip, I had several meetings plus the three-day prayer and fasting gathering and I was expecting a miracle of $5,000. Whether it came while I was in New York or would be waiting for me at home, I knew it would happen. In the natural, it seemed impossible. In the spirit I knew God could do it.

On Thursday afternoon the prayer and fasting gathering started with an intercessory prayer meeting. The numbers were smaller than last year but the Spirit of the Lord was truly sweet and precious. It ministered to all who came expecting to see God.

At the beginning of the week during this time in New York, I felt the Holy Spirit was grieved, because of the lack of interest of the American people to come to this type of meeting. They will go to dinner meetings in large numbers, where they do not really have to face God. At a meeting such as prayer and fasting, people don't want to come, humble themselves, and lay down their lives to seek God. Many are called but few are chosen to pay the price required for such a mission.

As the meeting progressed, the burden of God for America increased within me. There are so many hurting people in America, yet they do not know how to become free and stay free through prayer and fasting.

Friday evening, the Spirit of the Lord moved mightily in the midst of the meeting. I was ready to preach, but the Lord stopped me. He wanted to minister in a special way to the many hurts of the people. He directed me to a person who was hopeless and depressed about the future. Without a special touch from God, eventually this person was planning to end her life. God proved himself faithful to all of us who came to fast and pray and to seek Him. The rest of the evening God ministered to the needs of the people with words of knowledge and prophesy. It was awesome to see how much God loved us.

Later that Friday night, I had a dream. In the dream, in the chapel, where we held intercessory prayer meetings each morning, I saw women decorating. "What are you doing?" I asked. They answered to me that they were decorating for a birthday party. "Oh yes!" I said, with excitement in my voice. Then I woke up. Right away I knew something good was going to happen on the third day of our fasting.

Before the intercessory meeting, God gave me a word to preach. ***Rev. 3:14-22*** was the text I was to use revealing the condition of the Laodicean church. They were lukewarm, half-hearted, poor, wretched, naked and blind. This is the condition of America today, yet people don't realize this and fail to see that God wants them to repent.

Usually, at intercessory prayer meetings, I give a few scriptures and encourage them to pray on their own and then come together and pray for the nation, each on representing their own state, town and church. I normally don't preach at an intercession meeting, but I wanted to allow the Holy Spirit to control me and do whatever God wanted accomplished. As I continued to share, my heart ached and I began to weep uncontrollably for the hurting people in America and for the sins of the nation. The Spirit began to convict hearts in the room, and all those present began to weep and repent for their own sins and the sins of America. During the meeting, people asked me what they could do to help so my ministry could continue. Many people committed themselves to pray and to help financially monthly or as the Lord directed them, so this ministry could reach every corner of America.

On that day, God birthed in many hearts to commit themselves to come to Prayer Mountain (the place where we held a three-day prayer and fasting gathering) once a month or as often as the Lord leads, to pray and fast for the nation and for my ministry. As the Lord had shown me in the dream the night before, we celebrated the birthday of a new vision for many to pray and fast for America. After they had found out that I needed the miracle of $5,000 to publish my new book ***"If My People"***, those who had money that day, gave to the ministry, and others promised to send the money later. I returned home and within two weeks I had more than $5,000 that the Lord had promised.

After the three-day prayer and fasting gathering was over, I was amazed at what had happened. God reminded me of my dream in the ocean and showed me what can happen when I totally let go of myself and trust the Holy Spirit to control my life and ministry. I was so excited to see that the Holy Spirit had control of my life and that I was only a vessel used by God.

As usual, I was physically tired after the three-day meeting and I slept soundly through the night. However, I kept hearing the words of ***Joel 2:12-13 (NIV)*** "Even now, declares the Lord, return to me with all your heart. With fasting, weeping and mourning. Rend your heart and not your garments. Return to the Lord your God, for He is gracious and compassionate, slow to anger and abounding in love, and He relents from sending calamity." I woke up with these words in my mind but I could not understand what God was trying to say to me with this scripture. I had come to understand the scripture in 1986, and I used it many times while preaching to Americans to return to the Lord through prayer and fasting. For a while, I was known by Americans as the little Korean, Female John the Baptist. I could preach and pour out my heart to Americans to repent and turn from their wicked ways and have a personal relationship with God. Then, they could be healed, delivered from their bondages, and be set free to minister to the hurts of the people, and pray for the nation as Christians should do.

For sometime, I had not preached this message to Americans, and I began to wonder what had happened. I asked God to show me. Then He revealed to me that I had unknowingly gotten back on the water slide because I had allowed the fear of man to hinder me. I was thinking that the message would be too heavy for the people to handle. Without realizing what was happening I held back. As the revelation hit me I bowed before the Lord and repented of my sins. The Lord comforted, ministered to me and reminded me that He had placed the burden and had called me to wake up America. He reassured me that the only way I can be full of His anointing to do this ministry is to completely commit myself to Him and His Spirit. This will allow Him to be in control of the ministry and the Holy Spirit will enable me to do the work of the ministry.

As I recommitted myself to the Lord, then He reminded me of something He had shown me in one of the earlier gatherings. It was a dream I had after Dr. Choi had gone to be with Jesus. In the dream, Dr. Choi and I were standing before the President. The President gave her a paper and she in turn gave the paper to me. Then I woke up. I knew this dream meant something, but I never understood the complete meaning until now. As a light hit my whole being, I began to understand and see the whole picture of Gods purpose in my life. When Dr. Choi could not fulfill her dream to see revival in America, she stood before the President who represented The King (our God). She then gave me the assignment to continue the work she could not finish. I was awed at what God had shown me regarding where I was going and what I was to do. God spoke to me clearly, "Do not fear man nor rejection, allow my Spirit to take you to the places ready for this ministry." I was also to pass on the gift imparted to me by God through Dr. Choi and I would impart it to many American people. He showed me He will use this book ***"If My People"***, to move people to cry out to God through prayer and fasting. He then will lead me and show me where He would have me to go.

Three years ago in the area of Buffalo, New York, God birthed in me the vision for three days of prayer and fasting gatherings in many cities and churches through out the nation that He would open for me to go. Seeing the vision birthed in the hearts of the people while I was in New York has encouraged me that the time has come for a mighty move of God calling His people to prayer and fasting in a Spirit of true repentance for their sins and the sins of America. The Spirit of repentance will bring in a great revival that will turn this nation back to God through the harvest of multitudes of souls into the kingdom of God.

Now God has given me a new vision. I am to pray regarding the timing to take Americans to Korea. By going to "Fasting-Prayer Mountain" in Korea, Americans will see how Koreans fast and pray to seek God. I can help Americans understand the disciplined life of Koreans with my ability to speak both languages.

Through God's faithfulness I have been able to turn my vision into a reality. At the time of completion of this book, the Lord had already given me instructions concerning my next topic for publication. As God has proven Himself faithful to complete two books for Him, I am anxious to follow His leading for the third. I thank God for His faithfulness to fulfill the desires of my heart. Glory be to His Name.

Additional copies of:

IF MY PEOPLE $6.00

Also available by Sun Fannin:

THE BAD LUCK BABY $6.00

Please add postage and handling $1.50

Tape list available upon request

Order from:

SUNSHINE MINISTRIES
106 CRANBERRY DR.
P.O. BOX 453
GREENFIELD, IN 46140
317-326-8658